The Emergence of Freedom

The Emergence of Freedom

Freedom

The Sciences and the Human Spirit After Darwin

James A. Barham

Description

Scientism is the reigning belief system of our time. It is the worldview that the natural sciences, as they exist today, give us a complete and sufficient understanding of all of nature, including ourselves. This book has two main aims. The first is to challenge eight key ideas commonly held by supporters of scientism: eternalism in the philosophy of time, physicalist reductionism, (hard) determinism, mechanism in biology, neural reductionism, psychologism, moral relativism, and technocratic statism. The second, and perhaps more important, aim is to provide a new, positive narrative that explains humanity's place in nature in contrast to the dominant scientistic narrative. The key concepts explored throughout the book are emergence, freedom, and spirit. "Emergence" denotes the universal tendency in nature for increasing quantity to lead to novel qualities. "Freedom" means nature's broad disposition towards ever-increasing autonomy. "Spirit" signifies the domain of reality created by human social interaction, language, and rationality.

Library Cataloging Data

The Emergence of Freedom by James A. Barham
212 pages, 6 x 9 inches
Library of Congress Control Number: 2024922119
ISBN: 979-8991-7040-07 (Hardcover), 979-8-89946-005-0 (Paperback), 979-8-9917040-1-4 (Digital)
BISAC: PHI049000 PHILOSOPHY / Nature

Publisher Information

Inkwell Press
2321 Sir Barton Way
Suite 140-1032
Lexington, KY 40509

Book Cover Design:
Poet on a Mountaintop
Album leaf; ink on paper with added colors
40 cm height x 85.75 cm width
Shen Zhou; late 15th century
Nelson-Atkins Museum of Art
Kansas City, Missouri, USA

The inscribed poem by Shen may be translated as follows:

> White clouds like a belt
> > encircle the mountain's waist,
> A stone ledge flying in space
> > and the far thin road.
> I lean on my bramble staff
> > and gazing into space
> Make the note of my flute
> > an answer to the sounding torrent.

—Richard Edwards, *The Field of Stones* (1962: 40)

Image used in cover design is from Public Domain:
https://commons.wikimedia.org/wiki/File:Poet_on_a_Mountaintop.
jpg

Table of Contents

When we come to be instructed by Philosophers, we must bring the old light of common sense along with us, and by it judge of the new light which the Philosopher communicates to us.

—Thomas Reid, 1785 (2002: 27)

The question which we have now to face resolves itself into asking how science which appears to be a whole, and intuition which appears to be a whole also, can be fused and united so as to form a yet more genuine whole, which shall embrace them both.

—Émile Boutroux (1912: xii)

A narrowing of the field of vision is the inveterate vice of philosophy.

—Nicolai Hartmann, 1926 (2002: 1, 106)

Whether we appeal to science or not, we should not embrace a metaphysics that makes mundane but significant phenomena unintelligible.

—Lynne Rudder Baker (2013: 73)

[A]lthough we are born humans, we must continuously learn to be human;

—Tu Weiming (1991: 451)

Only after cultivating virtue could learning be discussed. Today, learning is being discussed without virtue being cultivated. No wonder people point only to one thing while neglecting one hundred. The times are getting worse.

—Huang Zongxi, 1693 (1987: 41)

Acknowledgments

I have accumulated innumerable intellectual debts during the very long gestation and writing of this book. While I cannot thank all my intellectual creditors here, I must not fail to acknowledge three people who have helped me the most over the past couple of decades or so: William A. Dembski, Lenny Moss, and Phillip R. Sloan. Without their guidance, friendship, and patience, this work would not exist. I thank all three of them from the bottom of my heart. I hasten to add that none of them is responsible for my idiosyncratic views or for my blunders. On the contrary, they have all registered their strong dissent, each in his own way. That they have continued to support me and my work, nonetheless, is testimony to their gift for friendship and tolerance of dissent.

I also wish to give a special "thank you" to my former teacher and one of my oldest friends, Aron Zysow. In addition to his invaluable moral, and even material, support over the years, he has been a sure and much-appreciated guide in all matters relating to Islamica and Judaica. He, too, should be exempt from blame for my errors of fact or judgment. [*Note:* A few days ago I received news of the death of Aron Zysow. Aron was a scholar's scholar, whose learning—always worn lightly—was of extraordinary depth and breadth. Above all, he was the kindest and sweetest-natured of men. Aron was my honored mentor and faithful friend for almost 50 years. I miss him terribly. *11/11/24*]

I am grateful, too, to the late Tom Bethell for his generous support when the going got especially rough. I am grieved that he did not live to see this work materialize.

I owe a very special debt of gratitude to Chris van Hemert of Pella Public Library's Interlibrary Loan Department. I could not have carried out the research that went into this book without her invaluable assistance over the past eight years.

In addition, I owe a big "thank you" to Jennifer Finley of Inkwell Press for her highly expert and patient work on the preparation of the manuscript. A heartfelt hat tip, as well, to Andrew Moretz for his help with the Figures.

Many others have helped me by providing copies of hard-to-find articles or by sharing with me copies of their own publications. Some have served as my interlocutors for years, while others have given me detailed comments on drafts. I cannot record all their names here, but it would be wrong of me not to mention at least the following: Enézio de Almeida Filho, Oliver Barham, Chris Blum, Keith Buhler, Stephen DeRose, Alex Jech, Brian Pitts, Joris van Rossum, and John Watterson. I am extremely grateful to them all.

Finally, my most important debt is to my wife, Nancy A. Recchia, for her steadfast love and support over the past two decades.

Dedication

To the memory of my grandfather,
Cecil T. "Jack" Wiley
(1899–1989)

A Gentleman must be strong and resolute, for his burden is heavy and the road is long. He takes benevolence as his burden. Is that not heavy? Only with death does the road come to an end. Is that not long?

—Confucius, *Analects* 8.7 (1979: 93)

Preface

Herbert Spencer was right about one thing: the homogeneous is indeed unstable.[1] At least, that is what the physicists tell us.

Once upon a time, there was nothing but the quantum vacuum. A fraction of a second later, there was the quark soup. After that, the galaxies, stars, and planets were born. Then, the first living cells made their appearance. At length, a kind of almost hairless ape began to walk upright upon its hind legs.

After that, in short order, the following things arrived in the world: bone flutes and the Lascaux murals; the *Iliad-Odyssey* and the *Mahābhārata*; the *Republic* and the *Mencius*; the Parthenon and the Selimiye Camii; the *Metaphysics* and the *Shifā'*; the *Elements* and the *Brāhmasphuṭasiddhānta*; the *Enneads* and the *Tantrāloka*; the *Tattvasaṃgraha* and the *Summa Theologiae*; *Romeo and Juliet* and the *Love Suicides at Sonezaki*; "Spring Vista" and the first *Duino Elegy*; the *Dream of the Red Chamber* and *In Search of Lost Time*; *Poet on a Mountaintop* and *Wanderer Above the Sea of Fog*; the *Six Suites for Solo Cello* and the *String Quartet No. 15 in A minor*; *Pather Panchali* and *Ugetsu Monogatari*; and the *Almagest* and the *Principia Mathematica*.[2]

The question that has long haunted philosophy is how to understand the second sequence in relation to the first. The reigning

---

[1] *First Principles*, Part II, Chapter XIX (Spencer, 1937: 364ff).

[2] Homer and Vyāsa; Plato and Mencius; Ictinus/Callicrates and Mimar Sinan; Aristotle and Avicenna; Euclid and Brahmagupta; Plotinus and Abhinavagupta; Śāntarakṣita and Thomas Aquinas; William Shakespeare and Chikamatsu Monzaemon; Du Fu and Rainer Maria Rilke; Cao Xueqin and Marcel Proust; Shen Zhou and Caspar David Friedrich; Johann Sebastian Bach and Ludwig van Beethoven; Satyajit Ray and Kenji Mizoguchi; and Claudius Ptolemy and Isaac Newton.

ideology of our day, which we may as well call *scientism,* basically answers the question this way: The entities in the second sequence *are not real.* They are some sort of hallucination that forms no part of what scientists take to be reality (and they would know).

In this book, I attempt to vindicate the opposite response: The entities listed in the second series are *real,* just as real as those in the first series. Therefore, it is incumbent upon me—and whoever agrees with me that the creations of the *human spirit* constitute an ineliminable element of reality—to explain what the first sequence must be like, to render the second one intelligible.

Perhaps most importantly, assuming this task means attempting to throw light on the question of how human free will can have arisen out of a natural world presumed to be rigidly deterministic. I approach this problem by means of distinguishing different degrees of freedom, of which ours is simply the most advanced—the "freest," if you will. As one prominent contemporary philosopher has put it:[3]

> [W]e need to recognize that not even all free actions are created equal—freedom itself comes in degrees.

One of the most important degrees or stages in that journey will turn out to be the advent of what I will call "natural" or "biological agency," the possession of which I claim is identical with the condition of being alive. One of the main tasks of this book will be the careful elucidation of this and closely related concepts.

This book has grown out of my doctoral dissertation,[4] in which I argued that teleology in biology is objectively real, and that there are cogent reasons for ascribing natural agency to living beings as such. Chapter 5 of the present book develops the argument of the dissertation in greater depth. It constitutes the conceptual axis upon which all the other chapters turn.[5]

Chapters 2 through 4 discuss the factors upstream of life that have conditioned its appearance. These chapters lay out views on time and change, reduction and emergence, causal determination and agency,

---

[3] O'Connor (2009: 199).

[4] Barham (2011).

[5] More recently, I have refined my conception of natural agency still further —see Barham (forthcoming).

such that the empirical facts relating to natural agency can be given a rational sense.

Chapters 6 through 9 discuss the implications of natural agency for phenomena downstream from life. These chapters explore such matters as animal sentience, human rationality, language and sociality, free will, human nature, morality, political community, and natural law.

The evidence and arguments presented in this book are of two fundamentally different kinds. The first type of argument is negative, or critical. That is, they are advanced in order to *refute* eight specific claims or theses advanced by proponents of scientism. These are eternalism, physicalist reductionism, hard determinism, mechanism, neural reductionism, irrationalism, moral relativism, and collectivism (especially in its current form of technocratic statism).

The book's second kind of argument is positive, seeking to construct an overarching worldview with which to replace scientism's grand reductionist narrative. For no mere refutation by itself will ever defeat scientism, seeing that human beings crave something positive to believe in. The non-reductionist (or emergentist) narrative sketched herein aims to lay the foundation for an alternative conceptual edifice that would respond to this need.

I have been thinking about this book for a very long time. My dissertation—which, as I say, provides the basis for the pivotal chapter 5—already lies more than thirteen years in the past. However, I have been reflecting upon the problem of man's place in nature for a much longer time—in fact, ever since a chance encounter, nearly fifty years ago now, with the marvelous book *An Inventive Universe* by Kenneth G. Denbigh,[6] which first awakened me from my physicalist slumbers.

Around 1989, another happy accident of the stacks brought to my attention the collection *Self-Organizing Systems: The Emergence of Order,* edited by F. Eugene Yates.[7] This superb volume provided me with a method to work by. All of the essays I published during

---

[6] Denbigh (1975).
[7] Yates (1987).

the 1990s were written under the sway of Yates's "homeodynamic" account of teleology in living things.

Finally, sometime around 2005, a kind stranger whose name I have forgotten brought to my attention via email the remarkable textbook *Cells, Gels and the Engines of Life: A New, Unifying Approach to Cell Function* by Gerald H. Pollack.[8] This book gave me the courage finally to speak openly about a heretical idea I had been entertaining privately for some time, namely, that the *sui generis* causal powers of living beings depend essentially upon their material constitution, i.e., the living state of matter.[9]

Originally, I intended *The Emergence of Freedom* in its present form to serve as a sort of detailed summary of the encyclopedic work I envisioned in my *folie de grandeur*. However, the passing years have convinced me that the text should see the light of day anyway, if only because it seems increasingly unlikely that it will ever exist in any other.

I have attempted to make the book as self-contained as possible. However, there are a few places where I felt it necessary to indicate ways in which the text needs to be supplemented. To that end, I have compiled a handful of lists of issues for further discussion. Naturally, I hope others will find my project attractive and will extend it in these directions, as well as in others I cannot foresee.

Pella, Iowa
October, 2024

---

[8] Pollack (2001).
[9] Barham (forthcoming).

Note on Translations

Quotations from non-English sources are translated in the main text, with the original passages included in the footnotes (or *vice versa*). While I include references to standard English translations in all cases, I sometimes provide my own translations, as well. These are marked "—JAB."

1. Introduction: What to Do When "Our Best Science" is Not Good Enough

1.1. Refuting Scientism

The aim of this book is to defend a certain commonsense view of the human spirit and of the everyday world of medium-sized material objects out of which spirit has emerged. While the commonsense worldview I wish to defend will take on board the properly warranted conclusions of the natural sciences, it will also acknowledge the cognitive authority of ordinary human experience. More specifically, the worldview presented in this book attempts to legitimate the objective existence, not only of the human spirit, but of purpose, value, meaning, and agency as really existing biological phenomena which are essentially connected with the nature and existence of life as such.

All of this means that, from the point of view to be developed in these pages, the teleological and normative character both of the human spirit and of the wider biological world within which spirit is embedded cannot be properly viewed as "epiphenomenal," "illusory," or a mere "projection" of the human mind onto a reality restricted to the ontology of fundamental physics.

A comprehensive defense of such realities as teleology, normativity, agency, spirit, and so forth, if successful, would be of more than purely academic interest. That is because a world in which such commonplace elements of our everyday human experience are "debunked" as cognitively worthless would be a world in which human freedom and moral responsibility are nothing but antiquated myths.

It would be a world in which traditional ideas of human nature, flourishing, and virtue are only impediments to the global reign of "experts." I will refer to the picture of the world and humanity's place in it painted by such self-styled "debunkers" as the "scientistic worldview," or just "scientism," for short.

Note that scientism is not a collection of scientific findings, but rather a philosophical system. It is a metaphysical doctrine which holds that all understanding of anything whatsoever must be sought in the results of the natural sciences—or even just in those of fundamental physics. As Wilfrid Sellars famously put it:.[1]

> [I]n the dimension of describing and explaining the world, science is the measure of all things, of what is that it is, and of what is not that it is not.

Scientism has been a topic of growing philosophical concern for some time now, and many of the various specific claims put forward by its proponents have already received close, critical scrutiny.[2] In the view of some, the obviously self-refuting character of any philosophical doctrine which denies the very existence of value—and hence of better and worse arguments—is too obvious to bother with. Why, then, cover such relatively well-trodden ground once again?

My main motive for writing this book is not merely to show what is wrong with the various scientistic theses I discuss—though I will do that. Rather, it is to mount a comprehensive assault on the scientistic worldview across as wide a front as possible. Even more importantly, I will attempt to construct a positive account of the nature of the universe, including spirit, to put in in its place.

Obviously, this is a very tall order. Why stick my neck out to such an extent, when good work in contemporary philosophy is widely supposed to be as tightly focused as possible?

---

[1] Sellars (1963: 173). Sellars was of course alluding to the famous maxim of the ancient Greek Sophist, Protagoras: "Of all things the measure is man, of things that are that they are, and of the things that are not that they are not" (cited in Graham, 2010: 701).

[2] See, for instance, Clark (2016), de Ridder *et al.* (2018), and Williams & Robinson (2015).

For one thing, the idea that philosophy ought to be narrowly specialized on the model of the natural sciences is itself a thesis within the scientistic world picture I am opposing. But more importantly, the purveyors of scientism to the general public by no means hamstring themselves in this way. On the contrary, I suggest the widespread appeal of their work lies precisely in its sweeping narrative scope.[3]

Plausibly, one of the main reasons why scientism has gained so enormously in popularity in recent decades is because it offers a replacement for the grand narratives of man's nature, origin, and destiny that used to be provided by philosophy, as well as the world's great religions. Scientism functions much like a religion in addressing first and last things—matters which most modern philosophy (and too frequently, religion) do not any longer credibly address.

I submit that, given the deep psychological roots of scientism's appeal, no amount of chipping away at it around the edges is likely to have any lasting effect. Even a systematic refutation of the claims of scientism across a wide front will ultimately be of no avail in the absence of a more-convincing narrative of the cosmos and of spirit's place in it. If that is so, then a successful refutation of scientism can only come in the form of such an alternative positive vision. That is the fundamental reason why I have written this book.

1.2. Reforming Naturalism

1.2.1. Towards a New Philosophy of Nature

The present work, then, represents neither a uniquely scientific nor a wholly philosophical approach to the problem of constructing a worldview more adequate to all the phenomena associated with the human spirit. Rather, it triangulates between the natural sciences and philosophy. While of course utilizing techniques of analytic

---

[3] The number of books promoting a comprehensive scientistic vision to a popular audience is legion. I will allow one recent book by a cognitive scientist, Spivey (2020), to stand in for the genre as a whole. This text is especially interesting because the synthesis it advances is based on some of the same empirical work in neuroscience and evolutionary ecology that I will be relying on, as well. I will endeavor to show that the same empirical findings provide greater warrant for a worldview diametrically opposed to scientism.

philosophy, it is essentially a work of *synthetic philosophy* intended to be judged by the standards of the natural sciences—on the basis of empirical (including phenomenological) evidence, inference to the best explanation, and overall coherence. In this way, it seeks to provide an updated "philosophy of nature."

As such, it takes inspiration from a number of other projects.[4] For example, in its twin focus on the critique of scientism and on the philosophical interpretation of the well-founded results of the natural sciences, the present book is perhaps closest in spirit to works such as Čapek (1961) or Denbigh (1975), though it is broader in scope than they are. Bunge (1974–1989) is suitably comprehensive, but for all its emphasis on "systems" and "emergence," his multi-volume work assumes a fundamentally uncritical stance towards the natural sciences, as a result of which the treatment of everything downstream from biology in the later volumes veers off the rails into scientism.

Another source of inspiration for this book is traditional Western philosophy, particularly as exemplified by the Aristotelian/Thomist philosophy of nature (including man). Yet another is the philosophical anthropology of the ancient Chinese Ruist (*rujia*), or "Confucian," philosophical tradition, which is in many ways convergent with that of Aristotle and Aquinas. A third is our commonsense understanding of the world, which is also to a large extent (though not entirely) congruent with the Aristotelian/Thomist and Ruist traditions.

I do not adhere to any philosophical school, traditional or modern, in a doctrinaire way. As the great early Japanese Buddhist scholar, Kūkai, once remarked:[5]

> A poet should learn the styles of olden times but not imitate them; a calligrapher should absorb the spirit manifested in ancient works but not copy them.

To which he might well have added:

---

[4] For an insightful historical introduction to the philosophy of nature, see Leclerc (1986).

[5] Kūkai (1972: 4).

A philosopher should sit at the feet of the great thinkers of all ages but not call any of them "Master."

1.2.2. Excursus on Hylomorphism

That said, the Aristotelian/Thomist perspective has undoubtedly had the largest impact on my thinking, overall. For the record, I accept and employ in this book many of the basic Aristotelian notions, including objectively real potentiality, change, substance, essence, teleology, the tripartite structure of the human "soul" or animating principle (*psukhē*), human nature, the virtues, and human flourishing. I take all these commitments to be in the spirit of the Aristotelian/ Thomistic tradition, if not always in accordance with its letter.

One major feature of Aristotelianism I do not invoke in this book is "hylomorphism"—essentially, the idea that whatever is real is analyzable into two complementary metaphysical components, namely, "matter" and "form." For present purposes, I pass over the problem of what, exactly, neo-Aristotelian thinkers mean by "matter," the better to concentrate on their notion of "form." Recent defenders of hylomorphism often maintain that form is necessary to adequately account for what they take to be the fundamentally *dual* nature of reality.[6]

Now, it is of course true that we make an important conceptual distinction between a "thing" and its "properties." But, obviously, there cannot be anything without properties—a propertyless thing is unthinkable—any more than there can be a property without a thing (at least, from a naturalistic perspective). For this reason, it is far from clear what is to be gained by invoking the language of hylomorphism beyond what is already expressed in the Aristotelian concepts of "substance" and "attribute," and these, as I have said, I am prepared to take on board. Though only a conceptual distinction, not a real one, it is justified by its usefulness in theoretical discourse.

However, form serves another important function within Aristotelian metaphysics. Namely, it provides a unifying principle for

---

[6] Dual, though not *dualistic*, for on the view under consideration matter cannot exist independently from form, nor *vice versa*.

substances. There is no doubt that this time the Aristotelian concept refers to an objective reality—a generic unifying principle underlying substances. But, still, I ask: Does the concept of form represent this reality adequately?

I submit that it does not. The reason is that we already possess a more adequate concept corresponding to the generic unifying principle, namely, the physical notion of "stability." Trading "stability" for "form" would result in a net loss in conceptual clarity, not a gain.

Various proposals for cashing out the notion of form *qua* "unifying principle" in acceptably modern scientific garb have been put forward by neo-Thomists in recent years. Two of these are energy and structure. As to the first, one author has demonstrated that the Aristotelian notion of form is *compatible* with the scientific concept of energy[7]—to which I respond: What is the use of the new concept if it is merely redundant? Regarding the second proposal, I must agree with another author who has noted that such an abstract concept would inevitably lead to the proliferation of "mereological monsters."[8]

The only reasonable alternative would appear to be to interpret the generic unifying principle as a species of causation. That is, the unifying principle of a thing is immanent in its inherent causal powers. These powers are what make something the kind of thing that it is. From a physical point of view, the unifying principle encompasses all the interactions, internal and external, which collectively create the *stability* of a given system. That is to say, from a physical point of view, the unity of a thing inheres in the principle of its stability.[9] Additionally, in certain cases, one may speak of a unifying principle consisting in "downward" or "top-down" causation, which seems to be an even stronger type of unity.[10] For all of these reasons, in my view, it is most fruitful to look to the internal principles posited by

---

[7] McLaughlin (2022).

[8] Austin (2020a: 125).

[9] I do not take the term "stability" to imply "static." In fact, dynamic stability is also a kind of stability. Indeed, all stability would probably be found to be dynamic if it was probed at a deep-enough level.

[10] I propose that a better name for "top-down" causation would be *reflexive causation*. For further discussion of this phenomenon, see below.

the natural sciences to provide an adequate account of the generic unity underlying the order of nature.

In spite of my reservations regarding hylomorphism, I wish to acknowledge the significant influence of contemporary Aristotelian and neo-Thomist thought upon the development of my views, especially, the work of Edward Feser, Robert C. Koons, E.J. Lowe, David S. Oderberg, and the late James F. Ross.[11]

1.2.3. Concerning "Liberal Naturalism"

Insofar as this book aspires to present an updated philosophy of nature, one might say it ought to count as a species of "naturalism." However, "naturalism" as usually understood comprises two fundamental principles, only one of which will be accepted here.

First, naturalism assumes the "causal closure" of nature. This means that all appeal to any causal influence emanating from a transcendent or supernatural realm is to be rejected. For the sake of argument, I accept this as a fundamental methodological commitment in the present work.

To be clear, I do not claim that only "methodological naturalism" has intellectual legitimacy. By no means do I wish to align myself with dogmatic atheism. I simply bracket the issue of a transcendent, necessary ground of being for later consideration. This, of course, presupposes that inquiry into "pure nature" (in the Scholastic phrase) is detachable from the question of "the radical origination of things" (as Leibniz put it).[12] But that is a position that was once considered quite defensible by orthodox theologians themselves.[13]

However that may be, it seems to me that the potential gains to be had from a naturalistic approach to the questions of freedom and spirit outweigh the risk of prematurely foreclosing recourse to the transcendent. These gains fall under two main heads. First, one cannot know in advance how far human reasoning on its own, unaided by

---

[11] See, especially, Feser (2019), Koons (2022), Lowe (2006), Oderberg (2008), and Ross (2008). For general discussion of the neo-Aristotelian revival, see Lennox (2017).

[12] Leibniz (1989).

[13] See Long (2010).

faith, may be pursued. The astonishing success of natural science up until now surely gives us reason to push the naturalistic methodology as far as it will go. Second, by adhering to naturalism in the sense of non-transcendence one is better placed to properly engage with one's intellectual opponents, thus avoiding merely preaching to the choir—a besetting sin of much of the present-day literature opposing scientism.

The other fundamental meaning of the term "naturalism" as it is usually understood today involves the rejection of the objective reality of the human spirit and everything associated with it. This means that purpose, value, meaning, agency, and so forth are considered to be "reducible" to some ontologically more-primitive base, which allegedly entitles us to regard them as mere epiphenomena, that is, as so many ontological fifth-wheels having no bearing on the course of events in nature.

I do not accept "naturalism" in this second sense, for many reasons. First and foremost, it flies in the face of the evidence of our everyday experience. Also, to define naturalism as encompassing this second principle is to presuppose the truth of scientism. Thus, the second principle of "naturalism" as it is usually understood in contemporary philosophical discourse begs the question against the critic of scientism. I offer this entire work in refutation of scientism, and thus of the second principle of naturalism so understood.

Others, of course, have attempted to defend the human spirit and its works within a broadly "naturalistic" setting, by which they merely mean they adhere to the first meaning of "naturalism" distinguished above, that of non-supernaturalism.[14] They have done so under a variety of names. John McDowell, for example, employs the phrase "liberal naturalism."[15]

McDowell's liberal naturalism includes the idea that the source of the human difference is our "second nature"—that is, the socially mediated achievement of enculturation or education, also known as *Bildung*, that is characteristic of members of our species. There is much to recommend such a view, although it needs to be qualified

---

[14] See, *e.g.*, McDowell (1998), Nagel (2001), and Strawson (1985).
[15] McDowell (1994: 89).

by adding that what *Bildung* is to an individual intellect, the history of human civilization is to spirit. On that understanding, I would not at all wish to downplay the importance of second nature for understanding the human difference.[16]

However, the proponents of liberal naturalism and similar doctrines mostly avoid grappling with the deep difficulties involved in explaining just how the social character of the human species in itself introduces normative agency into the world, elevating our species somehow above the purely physical goings-on they suppose wholly constitute the "first" or biological nature of all animals, including ourselves. So long as the proponents of liberal naturalism pay little or no attention to the metaphysical underpinnings of human second nature, they cannot but be suspected by their scientistic critics of advancing a form of substance dualism that violates naturalism according to its first acceptation. Such a doctrine would by no means be entitled to the mantle of "naturalism" in any sense whatsoever. For this reason, it will be important to look more closely at the ontological underpinnings of McDowell's "second nature"—which is more or less the same phenomenal domain I refer to as "spirit."

To sum up this point, my approach to the philosophy of nature unreservedly accepts the first principle of naturalism—and with it the broad constraint of "monism," suitably understood as an integrated picture of nature that leaves no gaping holes—while explicitly rejecting the second principle. At the same time, unlike most other contemporary "liberal naturalisms," my approach seeks to provide a full metaphysical grounding for the human spirit.[17]

Such a philosophy of nature will be informed throughout by the natural sciences—but critically so. This may sound presumptuous. What gives philosophy the intellectual right to dictate to science? The answer is twofold. First and foremost, natural science overreaches itself in promoting scientism, which is not verifiable science, but philosophy. We are told over and over that we must accept the metaphysical picture provided for us by "our best science." But what should we do when "our best science" is simply not good enough?

---

[16] The notion of "second nature" will be explored in some detail below.

[17] See Nagel (2012) for discussion of the necessity for such grounding.

The answer is, surely, that we must exercise our reason in critical fashion to round out our picture of reality as best we can.

The other part of the answer is this: the formula "our best science" presumes that our present-day science, even if it might someday be improved upon, is already *adequate* to deal with the matter at hand. Otherwise, there would be no point in appealing to "our best science" in the first place. But taken as a general rule, that assumption is groundless. How so? Consider: We know that our current science omits large swaths of reality from its purview (at the very least, human consciousness and everything that depends upon it). But if that is so, and if reality itself is unified,[18] then "our best science" is manifestly *inadequate* to deal with those domains of reality. The real presumption, therefore, lies in the scientistic denial of the inherent limitations of the natural sciences as they are presently constituted.

E.J. Lowe has put the point neatly:[19]

> Metaphysicians cannot afford to ignore developments in scientific theory, but they only promise to render themselves foolish in the eyes of posterity by slavishly accepting current scientific orthodoxy.

In view of the foregoing considerations, my approach to the philosophy of nature might well be characterized as "critical naturalism," if that term did not carry with it unwanted Kantian overtones. Instead, I refer to the approach adopted in this book as "reformed naturalism."

Reformed naturalism does not attempt to "demarcate" the natural sciences from philosophy (and the other humanities). Even less does it suppose that such boundaries as may be drawn at present between natural science and philosophy must remain fixed for all time. Reformed naturalism simply claims the right to rationally criticize the supposed philosophical implications of announced scientific results that in fact lack proper empirical and rational warrant.

---

[18] What would it even mean to deny this? If reality consisted of disjoint domains, then surely we could never have any causal interaction with any of the other domains. But if that were the case, then we could never obtain any evidence for their existence, either. Why, then, believe in them? In any case, I stipulate for present purposes that reality is "unified" in the sense that it consists of everything with which we could ever causally interact.

[19] Lowe (2009: 8).

At its heart, scientism is the effort to shoehorn the human spirit into a natural science several sizes too small for it. Reformed naturalism must challenge scientism by assisting the natural sciences properly understood. The best way for the philosophy of nature to help the sciences is by rationally criticizing their methods, concepts, and presuppositions.

In short, the aim of the philosophy of nature along the lines of reformed naturalism is to help the sciences to expand their intellectual horizons in order to provide a fuller and more adequate account of reality.

1.3. Defending the Human Spirit

In this section, I begin to take up the challenge of providing a positive account of the human spirit with which to oppose the nihilistic doctrines of scientism. Such an undertaking cannot be a simple affair. However, I hope to make my basic proposal definite and clear enough to provide at least a foundation for further work. I will begin by explaining in this section more fully what I have in mind by the somewhat loaded term, "spirit."

English lacks a suitable word with which to name precisely this aspect or dimension of human experience. The word "mind" will not serve, for several reasons. For one thing, it conflates human and animal modes of cognition. For another, it skews human rationality in an excessively individualistic direction. But perhaps most importantly, it has been corrupted by scientism in such a way that it now carries with it a distinctly reductionist connotation. It is chiefly for this reason that I decided to employ the word "spirit" to designate the domain of being that is brought about by the human language faculty and is reciprocally shaped by it, in keeping with the way the term *Geist* has long been used in the German philosophical tradition. A *locus classicus* of this usage is the following passage from Hegel:[20]

> The basis of right is the *realm of spirit* [*das Geistige*] in general and its precise location and point of departure is the *will*; the will is

---

[20] *Elements of the Philosophy of Right*, §4 (Hegel, 1991: 35).

free, so that freedom constitutes its substance and destiny and the system of right is the realm of actualized freedom, the world of spirit produced from within itself as a second nature. (original emphasis)

I considered the possibility of using terms borrowed from Eastern philosophical traditions, such as the Chinese term, "*xin* [*hsin*]," or the Japanese term, "*kokoro*." These terms have a similar wide connotation, encompassing both intellection and perception ("mind") and intuition and affect ("heart"), as well as will. For this reason, both words have often between translated "heart/mind."[21] But I am, after all, an American, writing in English, working within the Western intellectual tradition. Within that tradition, terms *Geist, esprit, spirit*, and so on seem to me to be the best choice. And these considerations are reinforced by the social dimension of human conscious life upon which I will be laying special emphasis below, especially, in chapters 7, 8, and 9.

All of this is not to say that the individual human reasoner is not important. Let us refer to rationality—meaning the reasoning capability present in every normal, adult, individual, human being —as "intellect." My claim is that spirit and intellect are reciprocally dependent upon each other. In this respect, the relation between spirit and intellect is not unlike that between the so-called "cloud" and individual computers. While the cloud does not ontologically depend upon the existence of any computer in particular, it does depend upon the existence of some computer or other, that is, upon the existence of computers as such, in a generic sense. Without computers, there could be no cloud. Similarly, without individual intellects, there could be no domain of spirit. Moreover, just as there is nothing in the cloud that is not in some individual computer, so too there is nothing in spirit that is not in some individual intellect or text, present or past. Contrariwise, just as there is little or nothing in any individual computer that is not founded upon something in the cloud, so too there is little or nothing in any intellect that is not founded upon spirit.[22]

---

[21] For discussion, see Swanson (2018).

[22] In making this claim, I am not denying that intellects may be creative. Rather, I am affirming that intellectual creativity mainly consists in making new

Here is an attempt to pin down precisely what I mean by "spirit" by means of a homely example. Think of an entirely ordinary domestic situation. My wife and I and our dog, Marty, are all gathered in the living room watching a film on the television set—say, the Russian version of *War and Peace*.[23] My wife and I see Prince Andrei lying wounded on the field of battle at Austerlitz, looking up at the sky, marveling at the beauty of the heavens, and feeling the wondrousness of simply being alive. We are moved by the actor's expressiveness, by the director's mastery, and, above all, by Tolstoy's psychological penetration and artistic vision.

Meanwhile, Marty is lying curled at our feet. He looks as though he were asleep, but if someone knocked at the door, he would be up like a shot, barking his head off. As it is, he lies contentedly at our feet. The same sound waves impinge on Marty's ear drums as on ours. If he happened to look in the direction of the television screen, the retinas of his eyes would be irradiated by the same light waves as ours. And, yet, not only is Marty oblivious to everything that is happening over his head, as it were, his obliviousness to the world that my wife and I inhabit is congenital and irremediable. Marty will never know Prince Andrei—or Pierre or Natasha. It is not in his nature to do so. The metaphysical abyss dividing Marty from my wife and me is as deep as it is wide, and it is unbridgeable.

When I speak in this book of "the human spirit" (or just "spirit"), I am referring to the totality of this common mental world in which human beings are naturally equipped to dwell, but which is strictly barred to all other animals.

1.4. The Natural Sciences and Common Sense

To provide an adequate defense of the metaphysical underpinnings of reformed naturalism would mean writing an entirely different kind of book. However, it is necessary to say at least a few words about

---

connections between elements previously contributed by others. Metaphorically speaking, every intellect is an tiny island in the ocean of spirit.

[23] Sergei Bondarchuk, *Voyna i Mir* (1966–1967); the great novel by Lev Tolstoy was originally published in 1869.

the most basic presuppositions I employ in this book. I orient the discussion around the relationship between the natural sciences and common sense.

By "the natural sciences," I mean here the sciences as socio-logical realities, that is, as professional disciplines and as human achievements. By "common sense," I mean our ordinary, everyday intuitive understanding of the natural and human worlds. The main issue I wish to discuss is the apparent tension at the heart of the rela-tion between these two phenomena—a tension which, if unresolved, would undermine my entire enterprise.

On the one hand, the natural sciences have both grown out of common sense historically and continue to be grounded in common sense epistemically. Without an entire suite of native human cogni-tive capabilities, the natural sciences could not exist. Scientists could neither apply the empirical method (which even in its most sophisticated forms relies upon the natural senses, if only to take meter-readings) nor create competing theoretical explanations of the evidence and adjudicate between them (inference to the best explanation and reflective equilibrium both being largely matters of intuition). In pointing out these things, I by no means intend to im-pugn genuine scientific endeavor. I not only acknowledge, but greatly admire, the grand edifice that natural scientists have constructed over the centuries, brick by brick, through the assiduous application of four main cognitive and social innovations: (1) systematic obser-vation and experimentation; (2) the extension of the human senses by means of technology; (3) the extension of our innate power of reasoning by means of mathematics; and (4) the social organization of the natural sciences, including the inculcation of the so-called "Mertonian norms."[24] But all of this just goes to show the deep connection between the natural sciences and common sense.

On the other hand, many scientists and philosophers are fond of disparaging common sense, in the firm conviction that the findings of the natural sciences contrast sharply with its deliverances and ought

---

[24] Communality, universalism, disinterestedness, and organized skepticism (Merton, 1942).

in all cases to supersede them. This is the central core of the scientistic frame of mind.

I will discuss these two viewpoints on the relation between the natural sciences and common sense separately, beginning with some aspects of the positive view I believe we ought to keep in mind, then passing on to a refutation of the negative view.

Reformed naturalism, and indeed the philosophy of nature as such, is an effort to combine *everything* we know about the world into a single, comprehensive framework. This means drawing on *both* the natural sciences *and* common sense.[25] The continuity between the natural sciences and common sense is thus a condition for the possibility of the philosophy of nature—or, rather, for any comprehensive view of the world that is not scientistic.

But *is* such an endeavor as reformed naturalism in fact possible? In addition to what I have already said above, I would now like to point out two more reasons for believing that it is.

First, both the natural sciences and common sense share a commitment to metaphysical realism. Apart from some working in the farther reaches of quantum physics, and, perhaps, in cognitive neuroscience, the vast majority of working scientists are natural-born realists. They believe the moon is there, craters and mountains and all, whether they are looking through the telescope or not. Scientific research would have little point if it did not illuminate an objective, external reality. For this reason, working scientists tend to have little time for either epistemological skepticism or idealism. In this respect, at least, I believe it is fair to say that the typical natural scientist fully agrees with the man in the street.

For this reason, reformed naturalism seeks to go back behind the modern attitude to philosophy ushered in by Descartes and company, which assigned pride of place to epistemology. From the point of view of the classical philosophy of nature, knowledge of knowledge itself must be sought in the context of our overall understanding of the world and of ourselves. In a phrase, "no epistemology without metaphysics." Meaning that first we *use* our capability for acquiring

---

[25] For discussion, see De Caro (2015).

knowledge to understand the world, and only afterwards do we seek a theoretical understanding of the knowledge we have been using all along.[26]

It should be apparent, therefore, that taking a "critical" path in philosophy need not mean taking epistemology as our starting point. On the present view, "critical" simply means applying our rational faculty equally to all the deliverances of our subjectivity: both what is internal to that subjectivity (we may call this the "map") and what is external to it (the "territory"), as well as the manner in which what is internal is itself an element of what is external—the way a map is itself a feature of a territory (like the map in the zoo saying "You are here"). Thus, being critical in the current context means, above all, being ever alert to this three-way distinction, and doing one's best to disambiguate one's language in order always to make as clear as possible which viewpoint—map, territory, or map-in-territory—is being adopted.

To summarize, within the context of reformed naturalism, epistemology will indeed be "naturalized," albeit in a very different way from most earlier efforts that have marched under the banner of "naturalization."

The other reason for accepting the continuity between the natural sciences and common sense is the following. In keeping with the spirit of metaphysical realism, a commitment to employing common sense in the pursuit of a philosophy of nature ought to mean adopting the same frank and honest attitude towards philosophical problems that, at their best, natural scientists exemplify in their attitude towards scientific problems. Though they may wind up denying one aspect or another of common sense, scientists do not typically *begin* by denying obvious features of everyday experience, as if for the sheer intellectual sport of it. As James F. Ross once noted:[27]

---

[26] I of course acknowledge that nothing I have said amounts to a proper philosophical response to the epistemological skeptic or idealist on his own terms. I am simply, *qua* philosopher of nature, taking those topics off the table; the focus of this book lies elsewhere. For discussion, see Fuqua (2021), Reid (1997), Rescher (2005), and Moore (1993).

[27] Ross (2008: 79).

> I suggest it as a methodological principle that in philosophy one ought to reason from what one thinks is so, rather than from suppositions one merely entertains, at least until what one thinks displays inconsistencies or unpalatable consequences.

Charles Sanders Peirce put same point more bluntly:[28]

> Let us not pretend to doubt in philosophy what we do not doubt in our hearts.

Remember that common sense is just our natural stance towards the world, the conception of reality provided to us by our innate cognitive equipment.[29] The *representations* of reality that the natural sciences help us to construct may very well extend our knowledge of the real, but they can never merely replace it. And, moreover, as Fyodor Dostoyevsky once pointed out, we are not likely, if we are sincere, to mistake the one for the other:[30]

> Try to draw an apple and place it beside a real apple—which would you take? I daresay you wouldn't make a mistake.

Thus, because common sense is shared by the natural scientist and the man in the street alike, even the scientist who creates a representation of some domain of reality that lies beyond our unaided five sense, nevertheless knows—or ought to know—very well where his representations end and reality begins. Since, as we just saw, both these individuals are instinctive metaphysical realists—at least until they are corrupted by bad philosophy—most of my opponents and I will agree on this point. Moreover, seeing that common sense is, in the main, just metaphysical realism under another name, it seems that natural scientists really ought to respect common sense in the same way most philosophers profess to do. After all, what is philosophical

---

[28] "Some Consequences of Four Incapacities"; Peirce (1992a: 29).

[29] To be sure, for human beings, the deliverances of "our innate cognitive equipment" are strongly shaped by our cultural upbringing, or "second nature," as already noted. Even so, I believe it is tolerably clear that common sense is much the same across even the most diverse cultures, however widely separated in space or time, much cultural-relativist cant to the contrary notwithstanding. This claim will be supported in chapters 7 through 9 below.

[30] *Demons*, Part II; chapter 5: "Before the Gala"; Section 3; Barbara Petrovna to Stepan Trofimovich (Dostoyevsky, 2008: 377).

"intuition," if not common sense? For this reason, in many respects, the natural sciences and common sense make common cause.

On the other hand, as mentioned above, many scientists and philosophers are as scornful of common sense as they are worshipful of science. Therefore, I need to say more to explain why the philosophy of nature ought to be grounded in common sense. Let us turn, then, to an examination of the negative view of the relation between the natural sciences and common sense. There are two main cases to consider: advances in the natural sciences that are in *conformity* with common sense, and findings that are in *confrontation* with common sense.

By "conformity," I have in mind cases in which the advance of the natural sciences poses little or no challenge to commonsense beliefs. Ptolemaic astronomy is a case in point. Although it advanced human knowledge very far *beyond* the scope of unaided common sense by dint of the application of trigonometry to carefully collected observational data, it nonetheless posed no direct challenge to any of the ordinary beliefs of the man in the street. Such cases are, I think, instructive, but they are not of course dispositive. Therefore, let us set them aside. For present purposes, we are more interested in how the natural sciences may come into conflict with common sense.

With respect to confrontation, two possibilities must be distinguished: (1) common sense may *assimilate* a contradictory scientific finding by renouncing its former belief, which then becomes relegated to the status of a "superstition," "illusion," or some other form of error; or else (2) it may *reject* the contradictory scientific finding and continue to adhere to its original belief.

Several points should be noted in connection with the first option of *assimilation*. To begin with, the distinction between appearance and reality is already deeply embedded in common sense itself. We do not need the natural sciences to teach us that the deliverances of our senses may sometimes be mistaken. A stick in a glass of water will do as well. Therefore, common sense has no difficulty in assimilating an alternative understanding of appearances when truly warranted. Proponents of scientism often advert to clichés such as the formerly commonsense appearance that the sun revolves around the earth. Well and good, but what of it? It is not as though common sense did not take the Copernican Revolution in its stride. I remember playing with a crank-operated, toy orrery as a boy and gradually coming to understand the truth about the rotation of the earth on its axis and the revolution of the earth around the sun, and why the commonsense belief that the heavens revolved around the earth was an illusion. This realization hardly led me to question my instinctive belief in the reality of the external world, much less did it overturn all of my ordinary, everyday beliefs wholesale. Nothing is more "commonsensical" than coming to grasp how appearances may sometimes be deceiving.

The fallacy underlying the scientistic position here is the idea that our occasional need to revise our picture of reality provides warrant for the much stronger claim that our picture of reality is wholly mistaken and must be revised root and branch. The former claim is banal; the latter claim is absurd. Above all, the inference from the former to the latter does not go through.

Let us call common sense that has assimilated the findings of the natural sciences in some domain "enlightened common sense." The foundation upon which scientism bases all its pretentions, then, comes down to this rule of thumb: Enlightened common sense is never justified in rejecting any putative result of the natural sciences. But is this claim itself justified? To answer this question, we must explore the second possibility mentioned above, in which common sense *rejects* some purported finding of the natural sciences.

To begin with, it should be noted how radical the claim is that some commonsense belief is an "illusion." The very idea of an "illusion" involves rejecting the way things seem to be—that is, rejecting some deliverances of the senses, *i.e.*, empirical datum. As we have seen, enlightened common sense may sometimes have to condemn one of its own beliefs as illusory. However, the bar for rejecting empirical evidence ought to be very high. At a minimum, it ought to involve showing why the appearance to be rejected seemed so persuasive—that is, how the error occurred. And whether this can in fact be done will depend upon the details of the case. I maintain that the proponents of scientism are far from being capable of explaining commonsense appearances, as a general rule, in the way they would have to do in order to be entitled to dismiss them as illusions. And if that is right, then it follows that many putatively scientific results simply do not hold up under scrutiny by the cold light of reason. This is especially true of purported scientific results concerning life, mind, intellect, and spirit, such as claims that things like purpose, value, agency, free will, and moral responsibility—all phenomena whose objective existence is as intuitively obvious to us as that of stones or stars—are mere illusions. Therefore, I reject what I characterized above as the central claim of scientism—that enlightened common sense is never entitled to reject a claim put forth in the name of natural science—as entirely without merit.

Nevertheless, scientism does pose one important challenge to its critics. It asks: According to what criterion can we hope to distinguish between assimilable and non-assimilable scientific claims? Making out such a criterion and making it stick are essential to my project.

One could, of course, write an entire treatise on this question. But for present purposes I will simply say this: Any putative findings of the natural sciences which not only affront common sense, but are also inconsistent with the existence of scientists themselves, are *ipso facto* to be rejected. Such self-refuting inconsistency is irrational on the face of it. When scientists and philosophers tell us with a straight face that entities like themselves do not exist, or exist merely as epiphenomena, we are under no obligation to believe them. After all, by their own admission, the sonic vibrations they set going by means of their vocal cords have no purpose, value, or meaning, and so no truth-value. But if the vocalizations of such wraiths are neither true nor false, but meaningless, then we who are made of more substantial stuff have no good reason to heed them. The task of science is to save the phenomena, not to conjure them away.

In this way, we may distinguish between common sense that is potentially *revisable* in the light of scientific findings (becoming enlightened common sense) versus common sense that is *unrevisable* under any conceivable circumstances, because its substantial revision would entail the rejection of the human spirit and so of science itself. Such unrevisable commonsense beliefs may confidently be maintained in the teeth of all the mockery and the condemnation that the advocates of scientism have to offer.

1.5. What About the Copernican Principle?

Finally, I would like to remark on an alleged difficulty for any project like mine that attempts to understand spirit's place in nature in an ontologically serious, non-reductive way. This difficulty is alleged to flow from a basic methodological principle of the natural sciences. I have in mind the "objectivity" of scientific knowledge—that is, "objectivity" in the epistemic sense of that term.[31] Objectivity in this sense is basically that idea that the knowledge in question is universal for all human reasoners. It is not viewpoint-dependent, perspectival, culturally relative, or conditioned by anything other than universal human perceptual and reasoning capabilities. Thus understood, the very objectivity of the sciences is often held to depend upon an idea that has known as the "Copernican Principle," meaning, in a nutshell, that human beings do not occupy a "special" or "privileged" position within the universe.

Now, to the extent that this is taken to mean that the universe is ontologically independent of human beings, the Copernican Principle is really nothing more than metaphysical realism. As such, not only does reformed naturalism have no quarrel with the principle, it insists upon it. Indeed, we have already noted how the metaphysical viewpoints of common sense and of the natural sciences cohere on just this point.

Thus, we really ought not to suppose that the existence or nature of things which are not ontologically dependent upon us in any way can be metaphysically affected by our presence or absence.[32] Copernicus was right—the earth really does revolve around the sun, not the other way around. Humanity does not occupy the center of the solar system—or the universe—and that's all there is to it.

---

[31] As opposed to the ontological sense in which something may be said to exist "objectively" if it exists in its own right, offering resistance to our will.

[32] Obviously, our presence affects other entities *physically* in all sort of ways, but that is beside the point here.

On the other hand, if we stop there, then the Copernican Principle may easily be misinterpreted as saying too much. The trouble with it is that it ignores the many cases in which the existence and nature of things are ontologically dependent upon us. All the phenomena of the realm of spirit—including, but not limited to, social, moral, political, legal, artistic, intellectual, and many other phenomena—fall into this category. I will consider what these things amount to, and how they are related to one another, in chapters 7, 8, and 9. But in whatever way one interprets them, they are clearly not nothing.

Indeed, much of human existence is lived in close contact with, and under the causal influence of, the entities that inhabit the domain of spirit (where the term "causal" is interpreted suitably broadly as encompassing reasons). For example, the idea of the unification of the South Slavs under Serbian leadership was the reason why Gavrilo Princip pulled the trigger in Sarajevo on June 28, 1914, lighting a conflagration that engulfed all Europe. Ideas have consequences. It is evident that they are ensconced within the causal nexus of the world. And yet there would be no ideas if there were no human beings. So, in this instance to apply the Copernican Principle would be quite mistaken.

A closely related idea is the that of "privilege." This idea seems to be invoked in the name of some hazy notion of "equality." Yet the world as a whole is anything but egalitarian. As I will argue in some detail in chapter 3, all order presupposes "privilege" in the sense that certain events are allowed while others are forbidden. Thus, a ray of light travels a "privileged" path—in a vacuum, the shortest path consistent with the curvature of the space in question. And so on for all the laws of physics. The laws of physics just *are* ways in which certain trajectories are privileged over others, that is, ways in which the actual movements of a test particle are *constrained* in comparison to the totality of its possible movements.[33]

Thus, privilege is inscribed into the very heart of things. However, the exact way in which privilege in this sense is manifested in

---

[33] In technical terms, the particle's "phase-space trajectory" is "condensed" or "non-ergodic."

diverse domains of reality—including spirit—is something that will require close scrutiny.

The problem of freedom is highly intricate, being intimately connected to a host of other fundamental metaphysical issues. A glance at the Table of Contents of this book will reveal which issues I take to be the most important with respect to constructing a critical, scientifically informed philosophy of nature (or synthetic philosophy) capable of providing a more adequate framework for understanding the emergence of freedom culminating in the human spirit.

2. Time and Change

The past, the present and the future are ordinarily taken to be all facts of the same status, disposed in an imaginary time-line and mutually distinct like facts in different space-positions. It is an illusory simplification of a complex situation.

—K.C. Bhattacharyya (1983: 636)

2.1. The Problem of Time

In this chapter I will take up the question of the reality of change and the passage of time, focusing on a few well-known arguments advanced by some proponents of scientism, which purport to prove that change and time are illusions and that reality consists of a four-dimensional spacetime "block universe," in which "the past" and "the future" possess the same ontological status as "the present." Following the standard nomenclature, I will refer to the defenders of this position as "eternalists." Their opponents, then, maintain the objective reality of change and the passage of time, and thus of an ontologically privileged moment we call "now" or "the present." Accordingly, the literature refers to them as "presentists."

Why is the debate between eternalists and presentists relevant to the struggle against scientism? Think of it this way. If the block universe were the correct model of the world we inhabit, then time would be exactly like space. In that case, "time" would exist "all at once," just as space does, which in turn would mean that the future would "already exist" down to the smallest detail. Obviously, such

a universe would be utterly alien to any coherent conception of freedom, not to mention to common sense. For this reason, the positive
project of constructing an alternative worldview to scientism cannot
even get off the ground until the arguments for eternalism littering
the conceptual ground have been demolished and cleared away. This
effectively means the project cannot get underway until an alternative
understanding of change and the passage of time has been found.

Eternalists advance many arguments for their highly counterin-
tuitive position, but I will focus here on just the following three:

1. According to the Special Theory of Relativity (STR), the
concept of simultaneity—all those features of reality which
coexist with one another—is not an objective fact, but rather
is relative to a human observer, and thus subjective. But if
simultaneity is subjective, then so is the present. And if there
is no objective present, then the only objective conception of
time we are left with is the block universe.

2. According to the presently most-popular conception of truth
(the "truthmaker theory"), every true *truthbearer*—which I
will take to be ultimately reducible to an *utterance*—must
stand in a real relation to some existing state of affairs that
makes the truthbearer true. This state of affairs is known as the
truthmaker. However, if the *relata* that any real relation con-
nects must *co-exist,* as seems plausible, then the truthmaker
for any true utterance about the past (*e.g.,* "Socrates drank
hemlock") must co-exist with that utterance. But, at the same
time, this utterance must be later than the truthmaker, else
the utterance would not count as being about the past. And
the only way an utterance could possibly be "later" than its
truthmaker, while still "co-existing" with it, would seem to be
if we lived in a block universe.

3. Finally, upon closer examination, the concept of the "present"
appears highly problematic. As Augustine of Hippo pointed
out, if the "present" is defined as "today," the 24 hours which
compose this day cannot all exist together. Therefore, some
hours must have already passed and others must have yet to
occur. It does not help to reduce the duration of the "present"

to a smaller magnitude—say, a minute—because the 60 seconds which compose this minute cannot all exist together, either. Therefore, some seconds must have already passed and other seconds must have yet to occur. And so on, *ad infinitum*.[1] In the literature, this has called this the "whittling argument."[2] I will call it the "problem of the "vanishing present." It of course implies that "the present," understood as encompassing all that exists together, cannot have any duration at all, no matter how small. In that case, the only coherent notion of "the present" is that of a point-like, durationless instant. On the other hand, a real temporal interval can no more be built up out of durationless instants than a real spatial interval can be built up out of unextended points. Once again, the block universe looms as our only intellectual refuge.

2.2. Time and the Special Theory of Relativity

According to the conventional wisdom, the first problem—the argument from the Special Theory of Relativity (STR) to eternalism —poses the gravest challenge to commonsense presentism. In a nutshell, the argument runs as follows: Because the speed of light is finite, the velocity of a light signal sent from point A to point B will depend upon the relative states of motion of the transmitter and receiver at the two points. Since this is generally true for all transmitters and receivers wherever they are located, each receiver B will experience the signals it may receive together—thus defining a plane of simultaneity in space—somewhat differently from every other receiver. Thus, what one perceives as simultaneous becomes relative to one's state of motion.

Obviously, from an operational point of view this is all well in order and has been empirically confirmed in many different ways. As a piece of science, it is unimpeachable. However, as a piece of

---

[1] *Confessions*, XI.20; Augustine (2012: 297–298).
[2] Miller (1974: 133).

philosophy—and as an argument in favor of eternalism—it contains a glaring conceptual fault: It is all simply irrelevant. Why is that?

The STR is irrelevant to the issue between presentists and eternalists for the simple reason that it is a theory of what is *observable*, not of what *is*. The finiteness of the speed of light imposes a limitation on our ability to *know* what is, but that is an entirely different matter. The speed of light is irrelevant to the ontological fact of the matter regarding what things enjoy coexistence because what is the case need not have anything to do with motion at all. While the concept of time essentially involves change, change need not consist in "motion" or "movement," in the sense of change of spatial position ("locomotion"). The kind of change with which the concept of time is essentially bound up may just as well consist in the alteration of some inherent or "intensive" property, thus amounting to "qualitative change." But qualitative change, or "alteration," has nothing whatever to do with the finitude of the speed of light.[3]

In short, the argument from the STR to eternalism mixes up epistemological and ontological issues and is simply irrelevant to the problem of which states of things coexist. It is just intuitively obvious that at any given "moment"—defined as the advance of the "wavefront of existence" up to that point (see below)—there must be a unique collection of coexisting particular states of things spread throughout the universe, no matter how great the distances separating them may be. To say otherwise would be to imply that those parts of reality lying beyond the boundaries of human observation are ontologically indeterminate—a greater absurdity than which is scarcely imaginable. All of which goes to show the essential idealism of the eternalist point of view.

As the philosopher J.R. Lucas has astutely observed:[4]

---

[3] Aristotle makes a similar distinction between locomotion and alteration, though he is not entirely consistent in his use of these terms. Specifically, he distinguishes *alloiōsis* ["qualitative change"] from generic change; see *Physics*, III.1, 201^{a}10–19; Aristotle (1983: 2), and VII.3, 245^{b}3–6; Aristotle (1934: 229). His usual term for "generic change" is *kinēsis*. See, *e.g.*, *Physics*, III.1, 200^{b}26*ff*; Aristotle (1983: 1*ff*). This seems strange because the word also means "movement," in the sense of "change of place" or "local motion," *as opposed* to qualitative change. Still, the distinction stands.

[4] Lucas (1999: 10); see, also, Prior (1970: 248).

Knowledge may be unable to travel faster than the speed of light, but reality does not have to travel at all.

2.3. Time and Truth

The second problem concerning the relation between time and truth will require more detailed discussion than the first. Still, I will strive to keep the discussion as compact as possible.

The eternalist argument from truth runs like this: Every true statement is made true by a truthmaker. To make a statement true, a truthmaker must exist at the time the statement is made. There are truths concerning the past, but according to presentists, there are no existing truthmakers to make those truths true. Therefore, the presentists must be wrong, and the past must exist on an ontological par with the present.

The obvious rejoinder to all of this is that making the semantic tail wag the metaphysical dog in this way is nuts. It should be obvious that our semantics must grow out of, and cohere with, our metaphysics, and not the other way around.

Unfortunately, saying just this much is unlikely to persuade the eternalist. What is really needed is a full-blown alternative semantic theory. While I do not have one to offer, I do have a more modest suggestion to make, which is this. There is in fact no need to abandon truthmaker theory entirely. Rather, we need to modify it in a sensible way to fit the context of statements expressing truths about the past. One possible way to do this—which I invite those interested in this issue to explore further—is that part of the medieval theory of "supposition" (roughly, the theory of reference) known as "ampliation."[5]

---

[5] I must note that ampliation theory also served as the basis for a theory of truth for statements about the future and for counterfactual statements. However, special care must be exercised with respect to these further uses. After all, to assume that utterances about the future have a determinate truth-value is to beg the question against the presentist. Intuitively, statements about the past appear have an objective truth-value in a way that statements about the future and counterfactual statements do not. In any case, only past truths are of immediate concern to us here, and I will restrict my own discussion to them for the sake of simplicity.

What is ampliation? One simple definition is to be found in the seminal logical text, *Summulae logicales* [Summaries of Logic], attributed to one "Peter of Spain."[6] Believed to have been composed during the second quarter of the thirteenth century, this work achieved the status of a classic for the later Middle Ages:[7]

> Ampliation is the widening of a common term from a smaller supposition to a larger one . . .

Next, let us see how this idea was used in practice. For example, in his *De puritate artis logicae* [On the Purity of the Art of Logic], written most likely during the third decade of the fourteenth century, Walter Burley explains:[8]

> Thus, if 'Socrates *was* white' *is* true, then the predicate, under the same form and under the same utterance and formal signification, must at some time *have been* predicated of Socrates. For if Socrates *was* white, then 'Socrates *is* white' must have been true at some time. [original emphasis]

Writing in reference to Thomas Aquinas, Gloria Frost has expressed the same idea in terms more accessible to the modern reader:[9]

> [T]he cause of a past-tense proposition's truth is the same object that caused the corresponding present-tense proposition to be true when it was true.

Or, even more pithily, this time in Aquinas's own words as cited by Frost:[10]

> [S]omething *was* is true because *something is* was true. (original emphasis)

Finally, William Ockham, in the first part of his *Summa logicae* [Summation of Logic], written in about 1323, seems to foresee the

---

[6] The identity of "Peter of Spain" is much disputed. See the "Introduction" to Peter of Spain (2014).

[7] Peter of Spain (2014: 441). For discussion of supposition and ampliation, see Ashworth (2014) and Kann (2016).

[8] Burley (2000: 132).

[9] Frost (2010: 199).

[10] *Ibid.* (201).

modern eternalist critique of presentism from the present nonexistence of truthmakers for past truths:[11]

> The source of doubt here is the earlier claim that a term never supposits for something unless it can be truly predicated of it. But if Socrates does not exist, 'man' cannot be truly predicated of Socrates; for 'Socrates is a man' is false. Thus, the term does not supposit for Socrates, so that it does not supposit determinately.

What is even more remarkable is that Ockham then appears to shape his account of ampliation theory specifically for the task of meeting this charge:[12]

> [T]he response to this objection is that it is correct to say that a term never supposits for something unless it is truly predicated of it. But this is not to say that a term never supposits for something unless it is truly predicated of it by means of a present tense verb. Where it supposits for a thing with respect to a past tense verb, it suffices that the term be truly predicated of the thing by means of a past tense verb.

Supposition theory and ampliation theory, then—or some modern refinement of them—are means by which truthmaker theory may be modified in a natural way such that we may ascribe truth-value to statements about past situations and occurrences, whether or not we are in a position to know what that truth-value is.[13] In so doing, it makes the metaphysical dog to wag the semantic tail, as is only fitting.

In sum, the possibility of a theory of reference based on the medieval theories of supposition and ampliation disarms the supposed refutation of presentism based on the putative non-existence of truthmakers for past truths.[14]

---

[11] *Summa logicae*, I.72 (Ockham, 1974: 203).

[12] *Ibid.* (205).

[13] Contemporary authors who advocate something along the lines of an ampliation approach to past truths, without using that terminology, include Baia (2012), Kierland & Monton (2007), Sanson & Caplan (2010), and Tallant (2009).

[14] It should also be noted that the entire literature on the relation of presentism to truthmaker theory is vitiated by its failure to attend to the fact that reference to non-existent or non-actual things ("intentional inexistence") is a fundamental power of human language and thought as such and has nothing especially to do

2.4. The Vanishing Present

The third problem is harder and more serious than the first two. It represents a much deeper metaphysical enigma. On the one hand, common sense demands we affirm the reality of change and the passage of time—and so the existence of a privileged position in time we call "now" or "the present"—as well as the equivalence or identity between the present and existence itself.[15] On the other hand, a close analysis of the notion of the present—as Augustine already observed (see above)—appears to show that it cannot be real, because interpreted in a fully realistic way it makes no sense. Either (1) the present is too big, containing within it elements of the non-existent past and future, or else (2) it is too small, containing within it nothing at all— and so no ontological resources out of which the really existing things that make up the universe could be built. Thus, it seems necessary to break the strong intuitive link between the concepts of existence and the present. And that way leads by a short route to eternalism.

I am unable to discuss here these complex and profoundly perplexing issues in anything like the detail they deserve. The best I can do for now is the following. First, with Aristotle, let us rigorously distinguish between "change," as a part of the territory, and "time," as a part of the map.[16] One way of articulating this distinction is by saying that the fundamental *ontological* relation between states in a process of change is not "before-after" or "earlier than–later than" but rather "*from-to.*" The former relations are ways we have of imposing a mental grid upon an ever-changing reality that is better characterized in itself by the latter relation.

---

with the presentism/eternalism debate. Intentional inexistence will be discussed in chapter 7.

[15] At least, with respect to our most basic conception of existence—physical existence. Of course, entities that are ontologically dependent upon human beings ("intentional objects," *entia rationis* ["beings of reason"], and so forth) require separate treatment (see chapter 7).

[16] *Ouk ara kinēsis ho chronos, all' hēi arithmon echei hē kinēsis* [Therefore, time is not change, but the way in which change is measured—JAB], *Physics* IV.11, 219^{b}4; Aristotle (1983: 44). For discussion of time in relation to existence and change, see Gentry (2021), Ingthorsson (2001), and Radovan (2015).

Looking at the matter in this light allows us to make a funda-mental distinction between (a) the shortest-possible wavelength of the periodic cycling of a physical entity permitted by the laws of nature, on the one hand, and (b) our mental ability to imagine peri-odicities of still-smaller wavelengths, on the other. Interpreting our problem in the first, realistic, way, gives us an "atom" of minimal, unchanging, physical existence, which we may identify with "the present." Then, once set in motion, the present so defined may be glossed as the "wavefront of existence," that is to say, the farthest point to which the ever-changing sequence of "total physical states of the universe" (TPSUs) has so far advanced.

Obviously, the notion of the "wavefront of existence" is just a metaphor—an analogy—and no analogy is perfect. This metaphor of a wavefront is meant to conjure up the (two-dimensional) image of the outermost circular wave emanating from a stone dropped in a pond, or, better, the (three-dimensional) image of the outermost spherical shell of radiation emanating from a transmitter antenna. Probably, a more adequate metaphor for the developmental (or "evolutionary") process of the universe would be that of a growing embryo. As a metaphor, the developing embryo has the advantage of downplaying the element of locomotion that is central to the concept of a wavefront, but which is inessential to our understanding of existence and change. However, seeing that we believe anyway in the cosmic expansion subsequent to the "big bang," there seems to be no good reason to deny ourselves the vividness and clarity of the wavefront metaphor. There is another reason why I like the wavefront metaphor. That is because the image of a "wavefront" clearly distin-guishes my conception of change from the so-called "growing block" theory of time—the view that the past and the present are equally real, but not the future.[17]

It is vital to note that while for any given human being the wavefront of existence for him will always be fixed by his own existence, that is in fact an entirely trivial point. After all, when could I be expected to make my observations of the universe, if not

---

[17] The idea of the growing block, though not the phrase, was introduced by C.D. Broad (1923: 66–67).

along the particular wavefront corresponding to my own existence? The wavefront of existence has nothing essentially to do with human beings or their conscious experiences. It is by virtue of being physical elements constituting a small part of any particular given TPSU that we determine the "present" point of advance of the wavefront, and not the other way around. A given TPSU and its corresponding wavefront might be determined just as well by any other state of affairs or event whatsoever, such as, say, the impact of the meteor that created the large crater in Arizona. When that event occurred, the wavefront of existence had advanced by a long series of "from-to" transitions to such-and-such a point. Now that I am looking out on the red oak tree outside my window, it has advanced up to this point. My subjectivity is an essential aspect of my way of existing, but it is only an infinitesimal element within the vast, onrushing, perpetually changing series of TPSUs that constitutes the mode of existence of physical reality.

Now, unfortunately, none of this quite gets at the heart of the problem of making sense of the present. The next step, I believe, is to make a further distinction between the single, global "pulse" of minimal periodicity (the TPSU) and the inconceivably many, local changes that occur to individual material things. Each of these may be said to enjoy a separate, unchanging existence in between changes, which may vary in extent in comparison with one another, depending upon the nature of the changes involved. This would seem to follow from the idea of defining change as essentially the "from-to" relation. So long as there is no change from x to y, x may be said still to exist, albeit in a sense which is not quite the same as the sense in which the transition from one TPSU to the next defines a change in what exists.

All of this becomes increasingly difficult to conceptualize and to spell out in detail, but the moral seems to be this. Even a realist such as myself seems forced to admit that the notion of "existence" has two fundamentally distinct uses. I don't want to say that "reality is relative." Heaven forbid! But I believe I must say something like this: When we speak of "reality" or "existence" we are often speaking equivocally, sliding between the notion of the wavefront of existence up to a given point, on the one hand, and that of the state of a particular thing at or near that point, on the other. And these are by no means the same thing. Drawing on the German ontological tradition, I will call the former "*Dasein,*"[18] that is, being present, and the latter "*Sosein,*" being such-and-such a thing. Thus, while there is only one "present" in the sense of *Dasein* at any given point reached by the wavefront of existence, there will generally be many different local "presents" in the sense of *Sosein* surrounding that point.

Putting the point in this way makes it clear that the real solution to the problem of the vanishing present lies in understanding how an unchanging entity at one length scale can coexist with a multitude of ever-changing physical time-atoms at a much smaller length scale. Another way of saying this is to ask the question: How is it possible for a single thing (substance) to exist by means of being unified across many physical moments? Or, still better, How is *durational unity* possible? This, in turn, is tantamount to asking: What are the interrelations among being, substance, and process?

I hope to return to these difficult issues in the future.[19] For now, I will simply note that one interesting attempt to split the difference between existence as instantaneous and as eternal was made by the medieval Latin-speaking philosophers in the doctrine of the *aevum.*[20] This doctrine was developed to help conceptualize the nature of angels in relation to change and time. On the one hand, it was standard teaching that in their essential nature angels are changeless. On the other hand, they can have what we would now call "Cambridge-relations" with external objects. The idea of the *aevum,* or "aeviternity," was that, from an internal point of view, the angel's changeless substance constitutes an atom or "drop"—as Alfred North Whitehead liked to say[21]—of existence that is similar to God's mode of existence, namely, eternity. At the same time, from an external viewpoint, angels can stand in various relations to external things in

---

[18] On the *Dasein-Sosein* distinction, see Hartmann (2019: 106–107). Note that this usage long antedates Martin Heidegger and should not be associated with his subjective interpretation of *Dasein.*

[19] In that projected work, I intend to focus on the interlocking concepts (and phenomena) of being, change, substance, and process.

[20] Cross (2012), Fox (2006: 255–273), Porro (2001).

[21] Whitehead (1978: *passim*).

the ordinary way of beings that exist in time (temporality). In short, an aeviternal being both is and is not subject to change, both does and does not exist in time, according to the point of view adopted. It has characteristics of both modes of being.

Originally restricted to the mode of existence of angels, the notion of the *aevum* was later extended by Duns Scotus and others to substances in general. I submit that it may be fruitful to rethink the concept of the *aevum*[22] as a means of theorizing durational unity and so of unraveling the problem of the vanishing present.

At the end of the day, the various issues raised in this chapter concerning time must be addressed by a deeper and more wide-reaching inquiry into the relation between being itself and change, or, equivalently (as I believe), the relation between substance and process.[23] What we *call* the contrasting *explananda*, of course, is of secondary importance. The basic point, though, is simple. As Émile Boutroux once put it:[24]

> Stability, however, has not undivided sway. In the very heart of its empire appears, as an original primitive element, the working of a principle of absolute change, of creation, strictly so called; and it is impossible to draw a frontier line between the two domains.

I will not attempt to undertake this difficult task here. However, I hope to do so in the near future.

* * *

Having dealt, then, with three of the principal arguments advanced by eternalists against the reality of change, I will henceforth take it for granted that our commonsense understanding of change is basically correct.

---

[22] To be sure, we will also need to take into account changes internal to the aeviternal being, since the unity of substances is generally grounded in lower-level processes. For the medievals, this was not a problem, angels being unextended in space.

[23] Among the various recent proposals of ways to do this, I believe the most promising is Ingthorsson (2021: 106–122).

[24] Boutroux (1920: 159–160).

As the outlaw poet François Villon asked:[25]

Mais où sont les neiges d'antan?

Last year's snows have vanished. They are not tucked away into some inaccessible corner of the "block universe." They just melted. They are long gone.

Past things once existed, but they no longer do. And not to exist is to be absent. It is to be nowhere. Not any place at all.

---

[25] [O, where are last year's snows?—JAB]. The verse is the refrain from François Villon's "Ballade des dames du temps jadis" [Ballad of the Ladies of Times Past], a section of his main poem, *Le Testament* [The Testament]; Villon (2020: 110).

3. Reduction and Emergence

3.1. The Concept of Physicalist Reduction

The next thesis that is often advanced by proponents of scientism against our commonsense understanding of the world is "reductionism." "Reduction" and "reductionism" are highly abstract and somewhat ambiguous concepts, which can be used in various ways. Here, I am concerned exclusively with "physicalist reduction," that is, the idea that longer–length scale, more-complex objects and, more generally, so-called "higher levels" of reality do not objectively exist, but are mere projections of the human mind which may be completely accounted for in terms of the particles and fields of fundamental physics. In other words, the palpable objects that surround us in our everyday lives are in some sense superfluous. To the eye of common sense, they appear to be real enough, but to the more-refined eye of the high-energy physicist or the physics-minded metaphysician, they are not "really" real.

All of this is in the nature of a thought experiment. Its point is to show that everything above the fundamental level enjoys an allegedly inferior—indeed ever-diminishing—grade of being. Note that the claim is not that entities at higher levels do not exist *at all,* even in a highly attenuated sense. That claim would amount to "eliminativism," not reductionism. Rather, the claim is that macroscopic objects make no contribution of their own to the overall causal inventory of the universe. For this reason, reductionism is sometimes described as "epiphenomenalism." An "epiphenomenon" is something of no importance accompanying, but not comprising an integral part of, something else. The image of the whistle on a locomotive is often trotted out to convey the idea. The whistle does not contribute to the causal processes that power the locomotive. From the point of view of the locomotive itself, it is strictly irrelevant. Even so, it is there. It exists.

I note in passing that the concept of "levels" or "strata" of reality is hotly disputed by many metaphysicians, although it is mostly taken for granted in the natural sciences and in everyday life. While I have no space to mount a detailed defense of a levels-ontology here, I will say that I take the issue of levels to be primarily an empirical one. That reality exhibits different properties at different length-scales can scarcely be denied, anymore than the fact that much of the natural world consists of entities nested within other entities, not least in living systems. There is no need to make heavy metaphysical weather of this demonstrable hierarchical structure. Nor is it necessary to posit a single overall structure into which everything that exists must be slotted. It is enough to point to the indisputable empirical facts just mentioned to justify speaking of "levels."[1]

Moreover, I would argue that reductionism as a theoretical framework for understanding the world is inherently unstable. When pressure is put upon it, the concept of reduction tends to collapse either into a single-level "fundamental" ontology indistinguishable from eliminativism or else into a hierarchically structured ontology with different degrees of causal dependence between entities that are nevertheless all equally real—which amounts to "emergentism." But reductionism is not only essentially equivocal, it also borders on incoherence. After all, what reason can be given to explain why the universe should be filled to overflowing with useless fifth wheels? For these reasons, I will not waste my breath trying to refute reductionism directly. Instead, I will focus my attention in this chapter on analyzing the contrary doctrine of anti-reductionism, or emergentism.

---

[1] For a penetrating examination of the hierarchical structure of nature, see Hartmann (2012). Blitz (1992) provides a useful historical study of the same topic.

3.2. The Concept of Emergence

Now, it is certainly true that "emergence" is a concept that is at least as problematic as "reduction." It, too, is often charged with conceptual ambiguity, if not incoherence. More explicitly, a common definition of emergence mentions two properties that are widely felt to be in tension with each other, if they do not constitute an outright contradiction.

Emergence may be cast in the form of events or properties or things. Here, I will focus on thing-emergence, or, more euphoniously, "entity-emergence." Entity-emergence is usually defined as follows:

- Higher-level entities possess a degree of ontological *autonomy* with respect to their lower-level component parts.
- Higher-level entities ontologically *depend* upon their parts in some way—they do not just float free from their material base.

Therefore, what a theory of emergence must do, above all, is show how these two requirements can be made consistent.

Now, my basic response is that there is clearly no logical contradiction here. It is true that autonomy and dependence are contrasting concepts and if the claims were absolute, there would be a formal contradiction. However, that is not the case. On the contrary, the claims are qualified ("a degree of autonomy," "depend . . . in some way"), and there is no formal contradiction involved in saying that A is partially autonomous from B, while still depending upon B in certain respects. This is a garden-variety observation that is true of most any teenager. Thus, it should not be controversial as an analysis of emergence.

All of this means that the two claims are fundamentally empirical in character. Moreover, there is an abundance of evidence that they are in fact true of a great many natural phenomena.[2] I note in passing that one of the reasons for the widespread skepticism regarding emergence lies in an unfortunate equivocation in the way that too many philosophers employ the term. Many seem to believe that the paradigmatic case of emergence is human consciousness, conceived

---

[2] Blasone et al. (2011), Hueschen & Phillips (2024).

of in a dualistic manner. Now, if this were the central meaning of emergence, it would indeed be a wholly obscure, if not formally inconsistent, concept. But that is not what I mean by "emergence" in this book. While I do regard mindedness as an emergent phenomenon, first, I regard it as but one of many such instances, and, second, I do not view mind as immaterial. These issues will be discussed in chapters 6 and 7.

That said, there is still a considerable amount that remains to be explored regarding emergence—more than I can consider in detail on the present occasion. Here, in summary form, is a list of the main points that would need to be discussed in a more comprehensive study of these matters:

- First, we must be clear that, while "reduction" is primarily an epistemic notion, "emergence"—at least, in the way I intend it —is primarily a metaphysical concept. The purpose of the concept of emergence is to point to a real phenomenon in nature, which we may summarize as genuine *hierarchical structure* of "levels," in which really existing larger-scale entities are composed of smaller-scale entities.
- The hierarchical structures we observe today have been built up gradually over the course of cosmic evolution—that is, simpler entities bring forth more-complex ones as changes occur. Therefore, I take the distinction between "synchronic" and "diachronic" emergence to be of small importance. It goes without saying that all synchronically emergent structures have come into existence through a process of diachronic emergence.
- Higher-level entities are indeed ontologically dependent upon lower-level entities. Without their parts, wholes would not exist. However, this would only imply that the parts fully determine the whole on the additional assumption of (hard) determinism. This assumption may be challenged (see chapter 4).
- In many cases, the whole exercises causal influence reflexively upon its own parts ("downward causation"). Thus, a whole may be said to be ontologically dependent upon its parts without being fully determined by them.

- Regarding the "autonomy" condition: Nothing is wholly autonomous apart from the universe as a whole.[3] So, what we clearly mean when we ascribe "autonomy" to emergent entities is only *partial* autonomy, not complete autonomy.
- I submit that the concepts of *stability* and *novelty* capture what we really mean by "emergence" much better than the term "autonomy."
- Higher-level wholes are best understood as coming into being through the Aristotelian notion of a *unifying principle* which underlies their stability. Stable systems, by definition, are relatively insensitive to causal influences at the lower hierarchical level of their physical base. That is what makes them stable. The notion of stability captures most of what we want from the notion of "autonomy," and does so in a way that dispels the air of mystery surrounding the latter term.
- We must distinguish between "resultant" wholes, or "aggregates," which lack an internal unifying principle, stability, and downward causation, on the one hand, and emergent wholes, or "emergents," on the other.
- In the case of emergents, the facts of stability and downward causation mean that there will be no simple (one-to-one) relation of causal dependence running between the lower and upper levels, in either direction. Instead, there will be highly nonlinear networks of causal *interactions*, running both ways.
- Regarding the idea of novelty, let us take a step back and look once again at the notion of change already discussed in chapter 2. The concept of "change" implies the coming-into-existence of a difference in something in some respect. If there is no difference of any kind, there is no change.
- The concept of "difference" implies the continuing existence of something underlying change. Otherwise, there is no answer to the question, "different from what?" Thus, when change occurs, something comes to be different in one respect, but remains the same in others. This is the traditional concept of

---

[3] As throughout, I waive discussion of the origin and ontological status of the universe itself.

"substance."[4] Without substances, changes would not occur within one-and-the-same world, but rather would be tantamount to the creation of new worlds *ex nihilo.*

- Change, or difference-making, can occur in two fundamentally different ways: quantitative and qualitative. There can be "more of the same"—that would still count as a difference with respect to the totality of what existed before. Or else there can be something altogether new—something hitherto unexampled in the world. This is the source of the distinction between aggregates and emergents.

- There is a theoretical link between the two forms of difference-making: namely, Philip W. Anderson's principle of "more is different."[5]

Let us look a bit more closely at this last point. The reason why more is different is quite simple. When there are more tokens of a type, there are more ways for them to interact with one another. Some of these ways of interacting will be impossible with fewer tokens. For this reason, some, at least, of the ways in which more-numerous tokens of a type are capable of interacting will, generally speaking, be different from the ways in which fewer tokens of the same type are capable of interacting.

One must be careful to distinguish the circumstances in which more-making leads to qualitative difference–making from those in which it does not. Generally speaking, this difference will depend upon whether the new entity that comes into existence is holistic in nature or is merely aggregative in relation to the previously existing entities (or some subset of them). In the former case, the novel entity will act as both cause and effect of the cohesion of (some of) the earlier entities into a genuine whole. As Alfred North Whitehead, with his gift for aphorism, once described this phenomenon:[6]

---

[4] "These distinctions having been made, in all cases of coming to be, if they are looked at as I suggest, this may be taken as definite, that there must always be something underlying which is the coming-to-be thing, and this, even if it is one in number, is not one in form," *Physics,* I.7, 190ª13–17; Aristotle (1970: 15).

[5] Anderson (1972).

[6] Whitehead (1978: 21).

The many become one, and are increased by one.

Whether the addition of being referred to by the phrase "more is different" is holistic or aggregative will presumably turn on the nature of the unifying principle involved and how it is related to the stability of the system in question. I take it that this will usually turn out to be an empirical matter, related to such physical phenomena as spontaneous symmetry breaking, critical points, and phase transitions.[7]

In this connection, if physical emergence continues to possess an air of mystery, then it is perhaps well to reflect upon Pierre Curie's famous dictum:[8]

C'est la dissymétrie qui crée le phénomène;

That is the fundamental reason why the world does not consist of just one kind of thing.

In addition to Curie's principle, however, there is the question of whether a given physical structure possesses a *unifying principle* by means of which the more-numerous tokens are brought together so as to behave in a *coherent, systematic* fashion. If there is, then the difference in the ensemble of the ways in which the parts are capable of interacting may sometimes be so great as to be tantamount to the coming-into-existence of a new type.[9] Let us call such a generic unifying principle the *principle of metastability* for the entity in question. It is this principle of metastability, acting in concert with Curie's principle, which lies at the root of the ontological hierarchy leading from the fundamental particles (bosons and leptons), to baryons and other composite particles, to atoms, to molecules, to stars, to crystals, to organelles, to cells, and so on.[10]

---

[7] See, e.g., Ellis (2016), Falkenburg & Morrison (2015), Gibb *et al.* (2019), Laughlin & Pines (2000), Morrison (2006), and Voosholz & Gabriel (2021).

[8] [It is the dissymmetry which creates the phenomenon—JAB]; Curie (1894: 400).

[9] See Brading & Castellani (2003), Castellani (1998), Georgi (1989), and Morrison (2006).

[10] It should be noted that this view makes "substance" and "process" into correlative, and not contrary, concepts. On the one hand, every individual "process," too, requires a unifying principle—which we may call a principle of *dynamical stability*—which constitutes some continuous suite of occurrences *as* an individual process. On the other hand, we know empirically that no "substance" is truly

I think that most physicists, chemists, biologists, and other scientists would be surprised to hear that the objects they study do not "really" exist. To be sure, the doctrine of "scientific realism" and the question of the "criterion" of reality are venerable topics of discussion in the philosophy of science. However, there is something approaching a consensus that if one can interact with an object—visible to the naked eye, or otherwise—then it must be real. This idea is often referred to in the literature (no doubt, with a nod to Dr. Johnson[11]) as the property of "kickability."[12]

Now, the reductionist will of course claim that, appearances to the contrary notwithstanding, causal interaction is always with fundamental entities. You can *call* what you "kick" a molecule or a cell, but all it really is is an aggregate of fundamental particles. However, this is demonstrably wrong. We can tell it is wrong both because science reveals to us that some objects exist at higher levels that simply do not exist at lower ones.

Take, for example, the phonon. According to quantum field theory (QFT), phonons are collective excitations associated with certain condensed-matter fields, such as crystal lattices. Phonons simply do not exist in forms of matter with shorter-range coherence than that found in solids and liquids. But are phonons real? Well, the workaday procedure in the toolkit of condensed-matter physicists known as "inelastic neutron-scattering" involves bouncing neutrons off them.[13] Hence, phonons are kickable. By that criterion, then, they are as real as Dr. Johnson's stone.

Another reason why the reductionist's position is demonstrably mistaken is because science itself is organized hierarchically. Why should that be? Clearly, because the world is organized that way and science seeks to get things right.

---

unchanging with respect to the principle of its stability at a lower hierarchical level. Rather, the latter is constituted by a suite of smaller individual processes at the lower length-scale. Thus, individual substances and processes are two sides of the same coin. For related discussion, see Austin (2020b).

[11] Boswell's *Life of Johnson*, Saturday, 6 August 1763; Boswell (1980: 333).

[12] Popper (1982: 46).

[13] See Gaulin (2012) and Vitiello (2001).

The above considerations show the fundamental wrong-headed-ness of reductionism. After all, the reductionist would have us believe that the ordinary, everyday objects that surround us—which form our *paradigm of reality*—are "less real" than the invisible particles of high-energy physics. Note that I am not saying that the fundamental particles are not real. I am a metaphysical realist, after all, which means I am also a scientific realist (however hedged around with qualifications that metaphysical stance may need to be). I am simply saying that no one has a legitimate reason for claiming that crystal lattices and rocks and human beings are not real, as well.

What about the unity of science? Some might feel that, while the kind of physical emergence outlined above might be attractive in some respects, it comes with too high a price tag—namely, the "disunity of science." Here, I will only say that it depends on what you mean by "unity." There is no reason why a satisfying version of the unity of science may not be retrieved from the viewpoint advanced here. It is just that such an epistemological unity will not be based upon a non-existent ontological unity consisting of a single ontological level populated by fundamental particles only. Instead, we must seek a suitably hierarchical form of epistemological unity corresponding to the objectively real hierarchy of nature. Such a conception of the unity of science will be based, not upon the reduc-tion of all that exists to a single, bottommost level, but rather upon (1) a unity of *principles*, not particles,[14] and (2) the *integration* of the entities existing at all hierarchical levels into a coherent whole. In short, our image of the unity of science ought to be that of a jigsaw puzzle, not that of a deductive argument.

Admittedly, emergence remains a challenging phenomenon. It is also a very general one. It may be that we will never be able to fully specify its essential nature, or will only be able to fully account for particular instances on a case-by-case basis. But it is tolerably clear that emergence also has at least a few generic features which appear to be universally applicable to all complexification and qualitative novelty of whatever sort.

---

[14] See Morrison (2006).

In any event, given the truth of our image of cosmic evolution from the quark soup to the human spirit, the reality of emergence cannot reasonably be denied. Hence, it is up to us to clarify and deepen our understanding of this supremely important phenomenon, which, in the final analysis, is nothing else than the creative principle of the universe. As such, physical emergence provides us with an indispensable concept without which the victory of common sense over scientism is unthinkable.

4. Determinism and Agency

4.1. Some Preliminary Considerations

The mystery and subtlety of the problem of free will have seldom been so vividly expressed as in a short reminiscence by the ill-fated French philosopher Jules Lequier (1814–1862) in which he lovingly describes the dawning of philosophical awareness in himself when he was a child, hesitating before the choice to pluck or not to pluck a leaf from a hornbeam tree (*Carpinus betulus*) growing in his family's garden.[1]

Needless to say, the problem of determinism and free will is a venerable one. Certain aspects of the problem as we know it today were already being discussed in Antiquity.[2] It was also of widespread concern within classical Indian philosophy.[3] The contemporary literature on the subject is vast.

What, exactly, is the doctrine of (hard) determinism? It was once well described by Charles Sanders Peirce:[4]

> Thus, given the state of the universe in the original nebula, and given the laws of mechanics, a sufficiently powerful mind could deduce from these data the precise form of every curlicue of every letter I am now writing.

---

[1] Lequier (1865).

[2] Bobzien (1999) and Dihle (1982). For notable episodes in the later history, see Harris (2005) and Hacking (1983).

[3] Dasti and Bryant (2013). It must be noted, however, that in Indian thought the emphasis was on explicating the notion of agency, as opposed to refuting determinism. From my perspective, this was a fruitful move, though I will not be able to pursue this interesting parallelism here.

[4] "The Doctrine of Necessity Examined"; Peirce (1992b: 299).

It is self-evident that if this vision of the universe is true, then our belief that we are free, morally responsible agents is false.

My purpose in this chapter is twofold. First, I discuss reasons for resisting the doctrine of (hard) determinism. Second, because it is not enough merely to refute determinism, I spend the majority of this chapter developing a reasonable form of agency to serve as the basis for a sui generis kind of determination, "agent causation."

I will not engage here with the immense professional literature on determinism and free will, but will defer that pleasure to a future occasion. Instead, I advance several general observations. First, setting aside metaphysical dualism, I note that there are only three *pure* positions on the problem of free will that have ever been clearly articulated by the mind of man (although many mixed positions exist). These are the three causal orders, so to speak, upon the foundation of which the human agent or actor may be supposed to be grounded:

1. *Acausality*—actions are uncaused, arising *at random.*
2. *Efficient (or event) causality*—actions arise by strict necessity.
3. *Agent causality*—actions arise within a framework of goals and hypothetical necessity for *reasons* that "incline but do not necessitate."[5]

The three philosophical doctrines based upon these pure species of determination—or "causality," in a generic sense—are known as "indeterminism," "(hard) determinism," and "metaphysical libertarianism," respectively. A fourth widely held position—"(soft) determinism" or "compatibilism"—claims to find no contradiction between efficient causality and free will, meaning that actions may be strictly determined and yet still be "under our control" or "up to us" in some meaningful sense. If this were so, then the problem of free will would never have occurred to anyone in the first place. Simply put, compatibilism is phenomenologically incredible. Therefore, it seems to me that there is no place in a proper philosophy of nature for this

---

[5] Leibniz, *Theodicy*, Part One, Section 45; Leibniz (1985: 148).

[6] *Critique of Practical Reason*, Book I, Chapter III, "Critical Elucidation of the Analytic of Pure Practical Reason"; Kant (1996a: 216).

"wretched subterfuge."[6] Any metaphysical libertarianism worthy of the name must eschew such dubious compromises.[7]

Finally, a fifth popular position, which would attempt to attenuate (hard) determinism by introducing elements of indeterminism, is hopeless inasmuch as it denies the strictness of determinism without providing any intelligible alternative explanation for our actions other than chance. But this will not do. Rather, it is essential to explain how free will is possible in a positive sense. If our actions are neither strictly determined nor wholly undetermined, then we who believe in free will owe a positive account of what precisely the control of our actions consists in. That is the appointed task of agent causation. But it is clear that this task can only be fulfilled by giving an account of natural agency that somehow coheres with the rest of our scientific worldview. That, accordingly, will be the focus of this chapter. The discussion will proceed in two stages.

As already indicated, I first examine the very idea of (hard) determinism, including whether it really holds sway anywhere at all, even in the inorganic realm. Afterwards, I explore the concept of *generic agency*, sharply distinguishing between free will in the proper sense of the term as an attribute of the specific form of generic agency I call *rational agency* and a much broader and more-primitive form of freedom deriving from what I call *biological agency*.[8] I take rational agency to be built upon the foundation of biological agency, augmented by the human capacity for responsiveness to abstract ideals, as well as deliberation in the light of those ideals.

These basic distinctions will be developed in the present chapter. Then, in the next chapter, I will proceed to a discussion of the nature of living systems *qua* agents, focusing on what it might mean for a biological agent to be physically instantiated.[9] After that, I will

---

[7] I am thus what Mele (2006: 95) would describe as a "hard libertarian."

[8] It should be noted that, while my strongly internalist interpretation of biological agency (Barham, 2011, 2012) shares features with some other analyses (see Barandiaran, et al., 2009; Skewes & Hooker, 2009), it also differs from the more widespread externalist-cognitive perspective represented by, for instance, Rosslenbroich, et al. (forthcoming), Sultan et al. (2022), Walsh (2015), and Walsh & Rupik (2023).

[9] See, also, Barham (forthcoming).

provide an account of sentient agency in higher animals in chapter 6 and of human rational agency—and free will, properly speaking—in chapter 7.

Some readers will wonder why I do not mention the question of moral responsibility above. The reason is that, despite some recent claims that the ethical question of moral responsibility should have priority over the metaphysical questions related to free will,[10] it seems obvious to me that this is wrong. Consider once again the young philosopher reflecting upon his own power either to pluck a leaf from the hornbeam plant or to refrain from doing so. This is an essentially metaphysical problem. There is nothing ethical about it. And yet it is clear that the child's power either to pluck the leaf or not is the *very same* power that Brutus possessed either to plunge his dagger into Caesar's breast or not to do so. Of course, Brutus's action was conditioned by a host of moral considerations that do not impinge upon the child's decision.

Note that the fact that free will is not absolute does not mean it does not exist. Like anything real, the power to act inherent in human rational agency is finite, conditioned on various contingencies, and limited and constrained in all sorts of ways. Like everything else that actually exists, one might add.[11] Nevertheless, the underlying metaphysical ground is the same in both cases. Therefore, if the child enjoys the power to do otherwise, then so did Brutus. And he does. For it is the fact that human beings are biological agents, in general, and rational agents, in particular (or so I will argue), that endows

---

[10] See, e.g., Franklin (2015).

[11] This point should be taken to heart by contributors to the immense literature on "Frankfurt examples" (Frankfurt, 1969). This type of thought experiment posits an agent who either brings about a state of affairs A or, if he intends to bring about a state of affairs B, is compelled by an intervener (a "mad scientist" or whatever) to bring about A, instead. Frankfurt examples purport to show that the agent is morally responsible for A even though he is *not* "free to do otherwise." But this is absurd. First, the very set-up of the Frankfurt example presupposes the agent's ability to do otherwise—after all, the whole point of the intervener is to block the agent from carrying through his intention to do precisely that. And second, how is a Frankfurt-style intervention different from any other contingency that limits our freedom? Why isn't it just obvious that if the agent does A voluntarily, he is morally responsible for his action, and if he is compelled *in point of fact* to do A despite his intention to do B, he is not morally responsible?

us with the potentiality for moral responsibility—for moral desert, praise and blame, and so on—and not the other way around. For this reason, I feel free to pursue here the metaphysical dimensions of the problem of freedom independently of the moral ones.[12]

4.2. The Problem of (Hard) Determinism

To begin, then, with respect to the concept of determination, I wish to make two brief points. First, as a metaphysical doctrine, determinism is often assumed to be proven *a priori* by means of the Principle of Sufficient Reason (PSR). To such critics, I reply that the PSR begs the question at issue. After all, it is not as though we knew the PSR to be true, at least in a form that entails determinism, independently of experience. Rather, it is a sort of induction from experience. But as such, it appears to be on shaky ground because it takes no heed of empirical evidence that contradicts it.

How is that? Passing by Heisenberg uncertainty, quantum indeterminacy, and related phenomena, let us instead proceed directly to the second point. Here, I would like to take issue with the widespread assumption that the "laws of nature" legitimate belief in determinism. Inasmuch as the laws of physics are mostly expressed in the form of linear differential equations, it is argued that each state of each particle stands in a unique, one-to-one, determinative relation to each of its immediately preceding and subsequent states. And what is true for each particle must be true for them all. In this way, the argument goes, the whole causal history of the universe—past, present, and future—is fully determined in all its minutest details. Note that this is a realistic picture, metaphysically speaking. Physical determinists are typically happy to admit that the future is largely unpredictable. They just ascribe that unpredictability to human ignorance, a concession which does nothing to undermine their metaphysical position. An infinite intelligence would be able to take in the whole causal history of the universe at a glance—whence the idea of the "block universe" already discussed above.

---

[12] I will briefly adduce some *sociological* evidence related to moral judgment in chapter 9, below, but that is an entirely different matter.

But consider again: What, exactly, *is* a law of nature, in this mathematical dress? Is it something immaterial inhabiting Plato's heaven? Is it something material but ethereal, like some kind of force field, only somehow floating free from matter? Or is it not, rather, a creation of the human intellect—that is, more a constituent of the map than of the territory? After all, there is a perfectly clear sense in which, before Isaac Newton, there was no "universal law of gravitation." Therefore, the law of universal gravitation and gravity itself are two different things. Namely, the former is a mathematical *representation* of the latter. Seeing, then, that the phrase "law of nature" is systematically ambiguous between epistemic and metaphysical senses, it behooves us to proceed with some care.

With this distinction in mind, we may pose the crucial question with respect to the determinism debate with greater precision, namely:

What is a law of nature in the *metaphysical* sense?

In formulating my own answer to this question, I will appeal to the recent literature which has reconceptualized the laws of nature as generalizations over the real "causal powers" (or "dispositions" or "propensities" or "tendencies") of material entities, or substances.[13] It is not, on this view, so much that "the laws of physics lie"[14] as that their full, exact, linear rigor is only an abstract approximation to the effects of the causal powers that drive the real world.[15] It should also be noted that the notion of "cause" itself is subject to a similar analysis. It would be question-begging to *assume* that "everything has a cause" in a sense that is incompatible with freedom.[16] Rather than view "causes" on the model of the laws of nature as expressing the underlying deterministic truth, we ought to view them as a heterogeneous assortment of influences which "incline without

---

[13] There is a burgeoning literature on this topic; see, especially, Anjum & Mumford (2018), Cartwright (1989), Harré & Madden (1975), Ingthorsson (2021), Roselii & Austin (2021), Steward (2012), and Williams (2019).

[14] Cartwright (1983).

[15] Early discussions of this idea include Boutroux (1920) and Peirce (1992b).

[16] This would be just another way of formulating the PSR.

necessitating," as Leibniz was wont to say.[17]

The physical chemist Kenneth G. Denbigh once put the point vividly, as follows:[18]

> Consider an analogy. A rigid steel rod of, say, 1 cm diameter is almost unbendable if it is only 10 cm long. But suppose it is 10^n miles long? Very minute impacts would cause it to wave about like a blade of grass. The actual constitution of matter is not such that there is complete rigidity over indefinite lengths; rigidity is an idealization. Similarly, I suggest, the "determination" of one state of affairs by another is also an idealization and is only to be taken as a good approximation to the extent that, in any actual instance, prediction over finite time intervals is found in fact to be a good approximation.

So much for the metaphysical doctrine of determinism. Of course, it is well known that free will cannot be vindicated solely on the basis of rejecting determinism. And introducing so-called "indeterminism" (chance) helps not at all. Our actions are free only to the extent that they belong to us. If we were forced to choose between necessity and chance, or some combination of the two, to explain our actions, then freedom of the will would indeed be an illusion. For this reason, making positive sense of the concept of agency is vitally important for the project of opposing scientism.

4.3. Libertarian Free Will and the Concept of Agency

In order to provide an adequate explanatory framework for understanding free will, we must turn now to the conceptual tangle of issues that is usually referred to as "libertarian free will." Above all, we must examine the notions of "agency" and of "agent causation" discussed by contributors to this literature,[19] which I find unsatisfac-

---

[17] *Theodicy*, Part One, Section 45; Leibniz (1985: 148).

[18] Denbigh (1981: 85).

[19] The nature of human agency is also discussed in the literature on "practical rationality," which is more or less separate from the literature on libertarian free will. The chief difference between the two lies in the fact that the literature on practical rationality debates the nature of agents while taking their existence for granted.

tory in several respects. For one thing, when it is not just empirically uninformed, it tends to invoke quantum theory in an unacceptable way. For another, it is very far from having provided a plausible account of what it is to be an "agent," and therefore fails in its primary task of articulating a defensible alternative to determinism, whether "hard" or "soft."[20] I will take a different approach.

I will examine some of the salient necessary (though not sufficient) conditions that must be met for a physical system to count as an "agent." More specifically, I will analyze and compare three different kinds of cases: (1) human beings with free will ("free agents"); (2) so-called "autonomous agents" in the most general sense ("generic agents");[21] and (3) naturally occurring autonomous agents ("natural agents"), which may be taken to be equivalent to living things.

I believe that each of my three accounts will be relatively uncontroversial, at least among those scholars who are primarily concerned with the literatures in question. Thus, I expect libertarian philosophers to mostly approve of my account of the necessary conditions that a free agent must meet. Similarly, scientists working in systems theory, cybernetics, artificial intelligence, and allied fields should agree with most of what I have to say about generic agents, while theoretical biologists will, I think, find my account of natural agents acceptable, at least as far as it goes. At any rate, I have drawn my

---

[20] Like Immanuel Kant, I consider "soft determinism," or "compatibilism," to be a "wretched subterfuge" that amounts to nothing more than the "freedom of a turnspit" (*Critique of Practical Reason,* Book I, Chapter 3, "Critical Elucidation of the Analytic of Pure Practical Reason," 5:96 and 5:97, respectively (Kant, 1996a: 216, 218). Similarly, William James called compatibilism a "quagmire of evasion" (James, 1956: 149).The problem of the freedom of the will is not verbal, it is metaphysical. In what follows, I will ignore the merely verbal "solution" proposed by compatibilism.

[21] Some will feel that I am abusing the term "agent" here, in effect begging many important questions. I am certainly taking an approach to the determinism/ free will issue that is not the usual one. However, this usage is by now well established in the natural sciences. Moreover, for me to call generic agents "proto-agents" or something of the sort would go against the realist, but non-anthropocentric, grain of the entire book. Therefore, I am going to dig in my heels and claim my author's right to use the terms "agent" and "agency" in my own way. Besides which, I am convinced that my approach will ultimately beg fewer questions than the traditional libertarian approach of proposing abstract analyses of agency that prescind from empirical considerations.

three lists of conditions from the three respective literatures with a view to presenting accounts that are as free from contention as possible. Finally—and this step will be both more original and more controversial—I will show that a free agent may be understood as a natural agent with an added condition.

While the discussion here will be conducted at a fairly high level of abstraction, it will prove useful once we turn to more empirically grounded examinations of life itself in chapter 5, of animal sentience in Chapter 6, and of human rationality in chapter 7.

To begin, then, I maintain the following propositions:

4.3.1. Free Agency

For a physical system to count as an *agent possessing free will* ("free agent"), it must satisfy the following requirements:

FA1: The system must possess *preferred states*, both internal and external, which we may call its *"goal-states."*

FA2: The system must be capable of *acting* in such a way as to attain its goal states.

FA3: The system's actions must be *controlled* or *guided* by the system itself.

FA4: The control of the system's actions must be at least partially *motivated by reasons*, not driven by efficient causes exclusively.

FA5: The reasons motivating the system's actions must be reasons *for the system itself.*

FA6: The system's reasons for acting must themselves be subject to *monitoring* and *control* by something internal to the system itself.

Of these six conditions, **FA3** and **FA4** have a special status. The bulk of the literature on libertarianism is focused on one or the other of them, which are often presented as alternatives. Following Kevin Timpe's helpful terminology,[22] we may give **FA3** the more-familiar name of the *source condition*, while **FA4** is equivalent to the so-called *leeway condition*.

The source condition says that an agent's power to act must reside within the agent itself. This seems indisputable, as any system whose

---

[22] Timpe (2017).

power to act derived from outside of itself would be a kind of puppet and no puppet ought to count as an "agent."

The leeway condition says that an agent's actions are not fully determined by the efficient-causal nexus within which they are enmeshed, but must in the last analysis be attributable to reasons. Note that to make a distinction between "causes" and "reasons" is *already* to deny determinism—which is the more-familiar way of looking at the leeway condition. That is, it is to deny that fixing the totality of the universe's efficient-causal conditions at a given instant uniquely determines an agent's actions, seeing that those actions are partly constituted by the non-efficient-causal influences we call "reasons." In short, the leeway condition says that the agent might have acted otherwise than it did on any given occasion, if it had had some to reason to do so. The agent itself is in control.

I note in passing that some care is required here, because the term "reasons" does not have precisely the same meaning in the context of generic biological or sentient agency that is does in the context of rational agency. Obviously, generic biological agency is not yet fully "voluntary" in the sense that sentient agency is, much less does it amount to the human kind of freedom (free will). Nevertheless, the most important distinction between efficient causes and reasons —namely, the latter incline without compelling[23]—unites all three forms of agency.

Now, I of course agree that the source condition and the leeway condition are both necessary conditions on anything's counting as an "agent." That is why I have introduced them as **FA3** and **FA4** above. Moreover, there is no reason, so far as I can see, why they ought to be regarded as mutually exclusive alternatives. Accepting both conditions seems to me to solve the difficulty raised by Timpe.

---

[23] O'Connor (2009: 213) further elucidates this distinction, in terms of human rational agency, as a distinction between sub-systemic *structuring* reasons instrumental to a goal and the whole-system *activating* reason, which is the decisive reason for the sake of which, upon deliberation, the agent's power of control is exercised. In other words, the activating reason arises out of the structuring reasons, but the source of the eventual decision and action nevertheless remains firmly grounded in the agent, understood as a substance. So, on the view under consideration—which I share—agent causation is a species of substance causation.

What of the other four conditions? They consist of the following commonsense observations. First, for anything to count as an "agent," it must be *non-indifferent* to its own possible physical states, according *preference* to some over others (**FA1**). Second, if one accepts this principle of non-indifference, then an agent must be capable of *acting* so as to attain its preferred states, or "goal-states" (**FA2**) and, third, the *reasons* linking those preferred states to those instrumental actions must be reasons for the agent itself (**FA5**). **FA5** is included on the list to exclude the possibility of a different sort of puppetry—an agent that acts out of its own powers, but only to satisfy some other agent's preferences. **FA5** is required to distinguish genuine agents from Kant's "turnspit"[24] and other, mechanical contrivances from automobiles to cruise missiles. Fourth, condition **FA6** adds the stipulation that a free agent must be capable of second-order monitoring and controlling its first-order actions. The reason for this condition will not concern us until chapter 7.

I hope that most metaphysical libertarians will recognize the validity of these conditions and agree that nothing that fails to satisfy them ought to count as a free agent. At any rate, I will assume that this is the case, for the sake of argument.[25]

With respect to my second list, I carry over the first two propositions unaltered from the first list. The remaining propositions go into more detail concerning the necessary elements of a generic agent.

I maintain, then, that:

4.3.2. Generic Agency

For a physical system to count as an *agent in a fully general sense* ("generic agent"), it must satisfy at least these requirements:

---

[24] *Critique of Practical Reason*, Book I, Chapter III, "Critical Elucidation of the Analytic of Pure Practical Reason"; Kant (1996a: 218).

[25] For a similar, empirically oriented model of free agency based on emergence and substance-causation, see Paolini Paoletti (2016). For a general defense of the metaphysics underpinning such models, see Lowe (2008). For an interesting critique of substance-causation, in favor of a process ontology, see Steward (2012).

GA1: The system must possess *preferred states*, both internal and external, which we may call its "*goal-states.*"

GA2: The system must be capable of *acting* in such a way as to attain its goal states.

GA3: In order to be capable of acting in such a way as to attain its goal states, the system must contain within itself a subsystem consisting of *effectors* capable of doing work, whether on the external environment or on the system's own internal states.

GA4: The system must also contain a *perceptual* subsystem capable of registering the nature and the valence of external states of the world and internal system states.

GA5: In addition, the system must contain a *cognitive* subsystem capable of doing, at least, three things:

    −remembering perceived world- and system-states.

    −inferring regularities in world- and system-states over time.

    −anticipating future world- and system-states.

GA6: That is, the system's cognitive subsystem must be capable of *comparing* an actual, present system state with a merely possible, future state *qua* goal state, then adjusting the effectors accordingly—all on the basis of inferred regularities.

GA7: Additionally, in order for the system to be capable of controlling its own actions, it cannot be tossed this way and that by local energy flows; rather, it must be partially *isolated* thermodynamically from its environment.

GA8: For this same reason, the system requires an *onboard energy supply* it can draw upon to do directed work, as needed.

Now, recall that we are discussing necessary conditions only. The question, then, arises: Are the foregoing conditions for a physical system to count as a generic autonomous agent also sufficient for all types of systems? For, if the list is sufficient, then all autonomous agents are generic in the sense that there are no differences among them that are significant enough to rise to the level of a categorical difference. In that case, our list of conditions is complete, giving us no grounds for distinguishing in any deep, metaphysical way between manmade machines and living things. According to this view— which is no doubt the majority view among scientists and scientism-friendly philosophers—robots and organisms are on an ontological par.

It is one of the most fundamental claims of my entire project that this view is mistaken. The full justification for this claim will have to wait for chapter 5. At this point, I will simply say that, phenomenologically, there appears to be a world of difference between generic autonomous agents as defined above, which would encompass both systems of human manufacture and living beings. The scientistically inclined will not, of course, deny that there is a big difference between manmade machines *as they presently exist* and living things. They will, however, deny that there is any in-principle or metaphysically deep difference between ideal robots and actual organisms. On the contrary, it is an article of faith of contemporary science and philosophy that an organism just *is* a kind of machine.

But what if that article of faith is in fact mistaken? I emphasize that I am talking about a difference in metaphysical category, not merely in how we conceive of things. Let us postulate, for the time being, that there is just such a deep and essential difference between our two categories of "autonomous agents," human artifacts and living beings. Assuming that the necessary conditions listed above for a physical system to count as a generic agent apply to both classes of objects, the difference must consist in some *additional* necessary condition upon living things. What might this extra condition be?

4.3.3. Natural Agency

The answer is not far to seek. It is just this:

> For a physical system to count as a living system, or **natural agent**, it must be an autonomous agent whose preferred states, or goal states, arise out of **its own causal powers**, that is, out of **its own material constitution**.

Let us call this the "material constitution condition" on natural agency.

Now, we may reproduce the list of conditions for a generic autonomous agent, with the material constitution condition added (in bold). The augmented list will look like this:

NA1: The system must possess *preferred states*, both internal and external, which we may call its *"goal-states."*

NA2: The system's goal states must arise out of its own material constitution.

NA3: The system must be capable of *acting* in such a way as to attain its goal states.

NA4: In order to be capable of acting in such a way as to attain its goal states, the system must contain within itself a subsystem consisting of *effectors* capable of doing work, whether on the external environment or on the system's own internal states.

NA5: The system must also contain a *perceptual* subsystem capable of registering the nature and the valence[26] of external states of the world and internal system states.

NA6: In addition, the system must contain a *cognitive*[27] subsystem capable of doing, at least, three things:

    –remembering perceived world- and system-states.

    –inferring regularities in world- and system-states over time.

    –anticipating future world- and system-states.

NA7: That is, the system's cognitive subsystem must be capable of *comparing* an actual, present system state with a merely possible, future state *qua* goal state, then adjusting the effectors accordingly—all on the basis of inferred regularities.

NA8: Additionally, in order for the system to be capable of controlling its own actions, it cannot be tossed this way and that by local energy flows; rather, it must be partially *isolated* thermodynamically from its environment.

NA9: For this same reason, the system requires an *onboard energy supply* it can draw upon to do directed work, as needed.

Now, let us compare our first and last lists, to see how well the more empirically oriented list (III) captures list (I) of abstract conditions on free agents.

---

[26] I do not list valence, or value, as a separate constituent condition on natural agency because it flows analytically from the notion of goal-directed action. I will discuss this point separately in a moment.

[27] On "cognition" as the instrumental coordination of actions with goal-states —and thus as a constitutive element of natural agency, or life. as such—see Albrecht-Buehler (2013), Fulda (2020), Lyon (2006, 2016), Miller *et al.* (2023), Shapiro (2021), and Van Duijn *et al.* (2006).

4.3.4. Comparison of Natural Agency with Free Agency

C1: **NA1** and **NA3** were taken over directly from **FA1** and **FA2**.

C2: According to **NA4–NA7**, a natural agent must contain structured subsystems which are collectively capable of *controlling* or *guiding* its actions in such a way as to attain its goal states. Together, these propositions fulfill the requirement that a free agent be controlled or guided by its own actions laid down by **F3**.

C3: The fact that a natural agent possesses preferred states (**NA1**) and is capable of acting in such a way as to attain them (**NA3**), together with the fact that its actions are controlled or guided *to that end* by its own structured subsystems (**NA4–NA7**) and the fact that the system is isolated from its environment and acts by accessing internal energy stores *as required* (**NA8–NA9**), all add up to the conclusion that the system's actions cannot be explained through physical causes exclusively; rather, its actions must be partially explained as being *motivated by reasons*, in accordance with **F4**.

C4: According to the material constitution condition (**N2**), a natural agent's goal states must arise *out of its own material constitution*. This is equivalent to **F5**, the condition that the reasons motivating a free agent's actions be reasons *for the system itself*.

We have now substantiated that our list of conditions on a natural agent captures the essence of a free agent, as well, at least with respect to the propositions **FA1–FA5**. But what about **FA6**?

Let us recall **FA6** to mind:

FA6: The system's reasons for acting must themselves be subject to *monitoring* and *control* by something internal to the system itself.

Nothing in our list of conditions on a natural agent corresponds to this condition on a free agent. Therefore, we may take **FA6** to be the distinguishing characteristic, or *differentia* (in the traditional terminology), of free agency with respect to natural agency. What this additional condition consists in, precisely, will be the central focus of chapters 7 and 8.

Before leaving the subject of agency, I would like to briefly discuss one more issue of some importance. Namely, as promised a few pages back, I will now review how the ideas of *values* and *norms* arise analytically out of the concept of *goal-directed action*.

I begin by recalling Thomas Aquinas's famous definition of *good* and *bad*:[28]

> bonum est faciendum et prosequendum, et malum vitandum

Note that, on this reading, value is relative to an agent's *nature*. Any object or state of the world which tends to *facilitate* the attainment of a natural agent's goal states constitutes a *positive value, i.e.,* is *good* for, that agent.[29] Similarly, whatever tends to *prevent* the attainment of a natural agent's goal states constitutes a *negative value, i.e.,* is *bad* for, the agent.

By the same reasoning, a natural agent's actions may be categorized as *successful* or *unsuccessful* according to the *criterion* of whether they attain their goal states. Note that such actions may be either *ultimate* or *proximate* (*instrumental*).

Moreover, if we assume that (1) object or world-state X is *good* (or *bad*) for a natural agent and (2) action φ *pursues* (or *avoids*) X, then it is natural to say that the agent *ought* (or *ought not*) to φ.

In this way, we can see that a natural agent's goal-states establish criteria, or *norms,* by virtue of either (1) their *fulfilment* or *non-fulfilment* by the agent's actions; or (2) the agent's *pursuit* or *avoidance* of an object or world-state through actions that are *instrumentally good or bad for* itself, *i.e.,* for its *ultimate* goal state (which—since we are talking about living things—is the continued maintenance of itself in existence as a token of the type of natural agent that it is).

Now, I realize that some readers may have considerable difficulty in hearing the terms "good" and "ought" in the above discussion in anything other than a *moral* sense. In response, I would contend that the material constitution condition on natural agency (**NA2**) is all that is needed to justify the language of value and normativity as I use them in a generalized sense in connection with the concept of natural

---

[28] [the good is what should be done and pursued, and the bad is what should be avoided—JAB], *Summa theologiae*, I^{a}II^{ae}, q. 94, a. 2; Aquinas (1948: II, 1009).

[29] Recall that we are discussing here the generic, panbiological sense of agency. Obviously, this statement will have to be qualified in various ways when adapted to specifically human agency.

agency. For this reason, it is imperative that I legitimate the material constitution condition itself. This will be the primary task and focus of the next chapter. However, as we shall begin to see momentarily, doing so constitutes a very difficult problem. In fact, it is one of the deepest and hardest of all the scientific problems facing us, though it is not commonly recognized as such. For this reason, I call it "the *other* hard problem."[30]

Let us now turn to it without further ado.

---

[30] Alluding, of course, to David Chalmers's "hard problem" of consciousness. See Chalmers (1996).

5. Life as Natural Agency

5.1. The *Other* Hard Problem

Consciousness, in the sense of feeling or subjective experience, is often referred to as "the hard problem" within the general mind-body problem. I maintain in this book that there is *another* "hard problem" that may be distinguished from that one: namely, "the life-body problem" or, as I shall call it, the problem of *biological agency.*

It *may* be that the two "hard" problems coincide in nature: that where there is life, there is rudimentary consciousness. But we do not presently possess conclusive reasons which compel us to believe that is so. In any case, agency is far more amenable to scientific investigation than consciousness, and for that reason alone is worth investigating in its own right.

5.2. The Phenomenology of Life

To make the case that even the most primitive forms of life exhibit all the characteristics of agency described in chapter 4, a motion picture is worth a multitude of words. Therefore, let us begin by watching this brief video clip[1] of a neutrophil (a type of white blood cell) pursuing a bacterium.

In this video, both organisms are clearly seen to be acting in a goal-directed, or teleological, fashion.[2] The neutrophil is pursuing something good for it: a meal. The bacterium is avoiding something

---

[1] https://www.youtube.com/watch?v=I_xh-bkiv_c.

[2] Note that here, as throughout, I use the term "teleology" to refer to goal-directedness, or purpose, in the internal, or local, or immanent, sense. In this book, I will not be using the term in the external, or global, or transcendent, sense of an entity exerting causal influence upon matter or minds from the outside, such

bad for it: its own destruction. These ways of speaking are inevitable. If we employ some circumlocution, we inevitably either beg the question or leave out something important. Moreover, phenomenologically speaking, we can simply look and see that these systems are behaving like generic agents. However, the point is not *just* phenomenological. It is scientific, as well. For, biologists themselves are increasingly willing to acknowledge the objective existence of the teleological, or purposive, organization of life. For example, a distinguished biochemist has recently written that:[3]

> Cells are multimolecular systems, intricately and *purposefully* organized at all levels from molecules and genes to physiology, functions, and durable structures. (emphasis added)

Knowing, as we do, that cells have been generated by other systems like themselves, we may go a step farther and say with some assurance that they are also natural agents. Moreover, cellular biology has confirmed the existence of organelles and other macromolecular structures corresponding to all the necessary subsystems we identified above as necessary to the existence of natural agents (effectors, perceptual and cognitive subsystems, and an onboard energy supply).

Furthermore, we may read value and normativity off the cells' obviously teleological behavior, as well. For the neutrophil, the replenishment of energy stores is an immediate goal because it furthers the more-fundamental goal of the cell's maintaining itself in existence.[4] Therefore, the capture and digestion of the bacterium is *good* for the neutrophil, hence something the neutrophil *ought to pursue*. As for the bacterium, like all living systems, it has the same ultimate goal of preserving its own life. Hence, being killed and consumed by the neutrophil is *bad* for it and is something the bacterium *ought to avoid*.

---

as Aristotle's Unmoved Mover or Pierre Teilhard de Chardin's Omega Point. For discussion of this distinction, see Lennox (1992).

   [3] Harold (2022: 169).

   [4] In the fuller discussion in chapter 5, it will be necessary to discuss the difference between an organism's maintaining itself in existence *qua* token and its doing so *qua* type. However, seeing that types cannot exist without tokens (unless Platonism is correct), the maintenance in existence of the type (reproduction) need not be our primary concern here.

In speaking of natural agency, teleology (purpose), value, perception, cognition, and so forth, I am already implicitly denying that they have any essential connection with consciousness, much less morality. So, I might as well make it explicit that I am using agential (*i.e.*, teleological, evaluative, and normative) language to speak of the behavior of these cells for the simple reason that it is *natural* and *fitting* to do so. That is, I am using the phrase "natural agency" to refer to the animating principle itself, in much the same way that Aristotle used the phrase *threptikē psukhē* ["nutritive soul"].[5] *How* natural agency can exist is, of course, a further question. But *that* it exists, I submit, is simply an observable fact, a *datum*.

It should also be noted that not all biologists have been reductionists. Several notable figures in the history of biology have taken something like the present perspective, namely, the idea lurking behind the concept of natural agency that life has an essence—a property that characterizes living systems, and only living systems, setting them apart from all nonliving systems. This essential property acts as the unifying principle by virtue of which living things are capable of *striving* to maintain themselves in existence and of *succeeding* in doing so at least some of the time. The French physiologist Xavier Bichat expressed this point pithily at the turn of the nineteenth century:[6]

La vie est l'ensemble des fonctions qui résistent à la mort

In 1920, the Hungarian physicist Ervin Bauer elaborated upon the same point in an instructive way:[7]

---

[5] *De Anima*, II.4, 415^{a}14–415^{b}27; and III.12; 434^{a}22–29; Aristotle (1993: 17–19, 72–73).

[6] [Life is the totality of functions which resist death—JAB]; Bichat (1994: 57).

[7] "[J]edes Körpersystem, das nicht im Gleichgewichtszustande ist und so eingerichtet ist, daß die Energieformen seiner gegebenen Umgebung zu solchen Energieformen in demselben umgewandelt werden, welche bei der gegebenen Umgebung **gegen** den Eintritt des Gleichgewichtszustandes wirken, nennen wir ein Lebewesen" (original emphasis in bold), Bauer (1920: 339). The translation is from Elek & Müller (2013: 130). For further discussion of Bauer, see Barham (forthcoming).

All living organisms are characterized by being a system that is not in equilibrium with its given environment and is so organized that it transforms the sources and forms of energy of its environment into such state that act **against** the establishment of equilibrium in the given environment. (original emphasis in bold)

In line with Bichat and Bauer, I submit that:

1. *In its essence, life is a state of organized matter capable of actively striving to maintain itself in existence, either as a token or as a type.*
2. *This capability may be appropriately termed "natural agency."*

In short, life is essentially an ongoing battle against the second law of thermodynamics.[8] Natural agency is the means by which life achieves its overriding goal of maintaining itself in existence.

Here is another way of saying the same thing: Life cannot be reduced to free-energy minimization. Rather, it essentially involves working *against* local energy gradients. All the non-living universe goes with the thermodynamic flow, whereas all living things, and only living things, do work *against the thermodynamic flow* in order to find a more-favorable environment. Thus, to maintain itself in existence, a living thing must do work on its environment *in a selective manner*. It is able to accomplish this feat by drawing down onboard energy stores (mostly in the form of ATP), which must then be replenished (whence the universal need to "eat," even if only sulfur atoms or photons). It is the need for this *selective* action—*admit* this molecule, *exclude* that one—which necessitates the perceptual and cognitive subsystems.

At this point, if not long before now, the skeptical reader is bound to be thinking: What about Darwin? Didn't the theory of natural selection put paid to my vitalistic-sounding presentation of the essential features of life as natural agency? In the next section, I turn to the question of whether modern evolutionary theory allows

---

[8] Naturally, the second law is still observed if we take into account the entropy-increase of the environment due to life activities, but that is beside the present point.

us to dispense with the concept of natural agency, understood in a literal and realistic sense.

5.3. The Philosophical Insignificance of the Theory of Natural Selection

To do justice to the issue of the philosophical import of the theory of natural selection, I would need to write an entire book, not a part of a chapter. But one cannot do everything and I hope to be able to show in a brief compass that Darwinian-style thinking is a scientifically superficial theory that leaves the deepest problem concerning the nature of life quite untouched. It is superficial in that it is the differential functional success of living things *qua* natural agents that explains their differential reproduction and not the other way around, as Darwinism maintains. Whatever Darwinism's utility may have been in the past, today it represents an obstacle to scientific progress. What is even more certain is that its *philosophical* significance is virtually nil.

From a philosophical point of view, the central feature of interest of the theory of natural selection has always lain in its claim to have reduced teleology to a combination of chance and necessity. With the final abandonment of God as an explanatory principle over the course of the nineteenth century, the evident teleological organization of living things stuck in the craw of hard-headed scientists and materialistic-minded philosophers. While living things might give every *appearance* of being natural agents—which indeed explains the survival of a vitalist strand of thinking in biology well into the twentieth century—tough-minded materialists, then as now, saw it as their job to explain away those uncomfortable appearances. It was against this intellectual background that Darwin was elevated to secular sainthood upon his death in 1882, complete with burial in Westminster Abbey.

The upshot of the foregoing is that the theory of natural selection was taken to demonstrate that teleology has no objective reality, but is merely "projected" onto living things by the human mind. If we accept Darwinism's core teaching that the appearance of teleology and agency in living beings can be adequately explained through the mechanical operation of the natural selection principle (random variation and selective retention), then there is no need to posit a separate principle to explain those unacceptable appearances. In this way, the idea of natural agency is rendered superfluous to our understanding of life.

However, this sweeping philosophical claim has fared poorly over the past three quarters of a century or so. First, in the aftermath of World War II, the theory of computation, the theory of information, and cybernetic theory all came along with their own mechanistic accounts teleology based on the concept of negative feedback. In 1958, this idea was rebaptized "teleonomy" by the botanist Colin Pittendrigh[9] and then popularized by the ornithologist-turned-philosopher, Ernst Mayr.[10] Pittendrigh and Mayr aimed to integrate the negative-feedback conception of teleology, or teleonomy, with the theory of natural selection. Mayr did this by distinguishing between the "proximate cause" of a functional biological trait and its "ultimate cause."[11] However, these biologists failed to realize that in giving a new label to the phenomenon, they were in effect taking back the claim that it did not exist. They did not like the look of the ugly pig named Teleology, so they put lipstick on it by renaming it Teleonomy. But a pig is still a pig, with or without lipstick. You cannot conjure something out of existence merely by renaming it.

Second, beginning in the 1940s, Barbara McClintock discovered the phenomenon of "mutable loci"—more popularly known as "jumping genes" and later re-christened the "fluid genome"—in the genetics of the maize plant. Out of her pioneering work has grown the modern fields of epigenetics and evolutionary developmental biology ("evo-devo"), which have completely transformed our understanding of the variation phase of the process of natural selection.[12]

---

[9] Pittendrigh (1958).

[10] Mayr (1965).

[11] *Ibid.*

[12] McClintock (1984); see, also, Jablonka & Lamb (2014), Moss (2002), Shapiro (2011), and West-Eberhard (2003).

Finally, in recent years, there has grown up a literature which takes an entirely different approach to teleology in biology. But even if teleology has been to some extent rehabilitated within biology itself, what about the charge that my position amounts to "vitalism"? Surely, the correct approach to living systems is *via* cybernetic theory, not a recrudescence of vitalism!

Well, no. As we have already seen, cybernetic theory may be well and good when it comes to artificial agents, but it entirely lacks the resources to explain natural agency. There is nothing in cybernetic theory which explains the material constitution condition —that is, how the material constituents of a physico-chemical system could ever assemble themselves into a system having a cybernetic organization. That is because steel, silicon, plastic, and all other simple inorganic and artificial materials—whether in themselves or in combination with one another—entirely lack the causal powers that would be needed for a cybernetic system's preferred states to arise out of its own material constitution, as opposed to being imposed upon it from without. For this reason, while cybernetics may be instructive in its own way, it cannot explain natural agency.

Moreover, "vitalism" is an ambiguous concept. It is often taken to refer to a form of substance dualism, in which "life," like the substance dualist's "consciousness," somehow detaches itself from matter and, as it were, floats free from it. But I hope the discussion of physical emergence above will have relieved any anxiety the reader might feel on that score. I take life to be an emergent feature of matter in the sense indicated in chapter 3. Exactly what that means, of course, will need a great deal of unpacking—and, frankly, further empirical and theoretical research. But I see no problem of principle here. "Vitalism" (or "neo-vitalism") will be an appropriate label for the present project, so long as it is remembered that this means only that life possesses its own essential nature and *sui generis*, emergent, unifying principle. I emphatically reject the charge that the emergence of natural agency amounts to metaphysical dualism. I hope it is obvious that such a contemporary form of scientific vitalism is a far cry from the quasi-mystical vitalism of the past.[13]

Lest it be thought that I have dismissed Darwin too quickly, or merely on the basis of changing scientific fashions, or by appeal to authority, I will now proceed to a summary of the reasons why the theory of natural selection must fail to do the philosophical job required of it by scientism, the job of reducing teleology to mechanism. First, I will state a general principle expressing an important biological application of the logical fallacy of *petitio principii*: what I call the "General *Petitio* Principle for Theoretical Biology" (GPPTB). Then, I will provide several specific applications of the GPPTB to important issues in the conceptual foundations of biology.

General *Petitio* Principle for Theoretical Biology:
To the extent that biological functioning is logically or chronologically prior to the process of natural selection—whether in the initial phase of random variation or in the subsequent phase of selective retention—to that extent does the theory of natural selection beg the question of the source of teleology and agency in organisms.

Applications:

- The theory of natural selection subordinates functional organization to reproduction, but, logically, something must already exist before it can be reproduced; thus, viable phenotypes must already exist before they can be "selected."[14]
- It is a well-supported empirical fact that reproduction is under functional control in all real living systems.
- We now know that genetic variation is not always "random," but is often under functional control.
- We now know that variants which lead to viable phenotypic traits—however they are produced in the phase of variation —are not incorporated into the organism "by chance"; rather, every phenotypic variant is actively assimilated to the pre-existing functional organization of the organism.

---

[13] *Cf.* Cornish-Bowden (2006).
[14] See Cornish-Bowden (2006: 487–488).

- It is this capacity for functional assimilation ("plasticity" or "adaptability") that is the real generator of phenotypic viability, and thus evolutionary change.
- Therefore, differential reproduction ("selection") is the *effect* of biological functioning, not its cause.

Throughout all the vast realms of physics and chemistry, we explain the existence of the entities we observe by invoking their unifying principles, by virtue of which they possess their particular form of stability. Only in the realm of biology—the domain of systems many orders of magnitude *more* complex than the most-complex forms of inanimate matter—are we told *there is no essential nature or unifying principle*. But this is now no longer credible, if it ever was.

It is not, of course, that the theory of natural selection is *wrong*, exactly. Rather, it is *superficial* and relatively insignificant, scientifically. Its *philosophical* significance is even less, indeed virtually nil. Accordingly, biology today still finds itself in much the same dead end as psychology did during the reign of behaviorism. In fact, *Darwinism is biological behaviorism*. Darwinian biologists treat the teleological organization of the organism as a black box in the same way that behaviorist psychologists treated the mind. As in psychology during the 1950s, in biology today further progress requires that we leave outdated ways of thinking behind. For this reason, any philosophy of nature that has a chance of successfully resisting scientism must be grounded in *post-Darwinian biology*.

What, then, is my alternative to the Darwinian explanatory framework? What positive account of the *other* hard problem—natural agency—do I have to offer? To begin to answer this difficult question, let us look a little more closely at what some physicists call "the living state of matter."

5.4. What Might an Organism Be, If Not a Machine?

So far as the presently known laws of physics and chemistry are concerned, life should not exist. And yet it does. That is the problem that must be addressed if we are ever to escape from the *cul-de-sac* of Darwinian thinking.

There are two broad possibilities. One is that the scientific key to understanding life lies far beyond our grasp in a way that is presently unimaginable. On this view, we stand today in the same relation to the necessary breakthrough in biology that would afford us a deep understanding of life as that in which physicists stood in relation to quantum theory in the late nineteenth century, before the path-breaking work of Max Planck. On this view, contented twenty-first century Darwinists are so many complacent Lord Kelvins.[15] Some present-day mainstream biologists are gingerly coming to this conclusion. For example, Franklin M. Harold has stated that:[16]

> I cannot shake off the nagging hunch that there is much, much more to the question of origins than is dreamt of in contemporary scientific discourse. If and when someone devises a persuasive scenario for how life came to be, it may be situated in a world radically different from the one we currently take for granted.

The other possibility is that we are already in possession of the key, but we have not yet discovered how to use it to open the lock of theoretical biology, because we have hardly begun to try in any serious way. Darwinism has acted as an opiate, dulling the acute intellectual pain that we ought to feel whenever we reflect upon the extraordinary nature of life. Instead of trying to relieve the pain by delving deeper into the theoretical foundations of the living state of matter, most biologists are content to go on filling in the myriad details of how natural agents are organized. They studiously look away from the

---

[15] In a series of articles published from the 1860s through the 1890s, Lord Kelvin (William Thomson) presented calculations of the age of the sun—and, by implication, of the earth—that he made on the basis of classical thermodynamics (which he had helped pioneer), in blissful ignorance of the existence of radioactivity. Kelvin confidently estimated this age to be on the order of magnitude of tens of millions of years. On this basis, he challenged Darwin's theory of natural selection. See Lindley (2004). If this is indeed our situation, it is a further question whether we *can* discover the principle we are currently missing. Seeing that the negative answer to this question (*"ignorabimus"*) is a counsel of despair, I will assume the positive answer.

[16] Harold (2022: 95).

impenetrable mystery that lies at the heart of biology: How *can* such a thing as a natural agent exist in the first place?

A critical reader might protest that what I say ignores the origin of life literature. But that literature—which is now entering upon its seventh decade and is based almost wholly on Darwinian principles—has been quite remarkable for its fruitlessness. It is safe to say that we are not much nearer to understanding how life is possible today than we were back in 1952, when Stanley Miller and Harold Urey demonstrated that amino acids could be created abiotically. To be sure, the abiotic creation of amino acids in a test tube was an interesting result. But with the benefit of hindsight, we can see that the Miller-Urey experiment did not lead us towards the sort of deep insight we need most. Rather, from these considerations, we may conclude that the unifying principle of life must be lurking somewhere in the immense gap between the chemically relatively simple amino acids, nucleotides, sugars, and fatty acids, on the one hand, and the macromolecular proteins, nucleic acids, polysaccharides, and lipids, as well as the entire menagerie of complex membranes and organelles, on the other.

That said, I must add that the news is not all bad. The fact is that there are now a number of very interesting proposals on the table regarding the essential nature of life that involve *condensed-matter physics*. I will not rehearse the details of those proposals here.[17] For the present, suffice it to say that the proposals I will be discussing in chapter 5 are based on the following combination of empirical facts and logical inferences:

- A living cell is *not* a bag of chemicals in solution; rather, cytoplasm is a gel-like state of matter.
- Therefore, the collective phenomena occurring within cells may be viewed, at least in part and at a suitably general level of

---

[17] However, I may refer the interested reader to Ho (2008), Kauffman (2019), Laughlin *et al.* (2000), and Pollack (2001). For the importance of the physical coupling of living systems with "ordered water," see Pollack (2013) and Watterson (2018, in progress). For recent empirical research in "quantum biology," which is far more limited in scope but still suggestive, see Mohseni *et al.* (2014).

abstraction, as analogous to the collective phenomena occurring within "active gels."[18]

- In that case, the unifying principles underlying gels and other condensed states of matter are likely also among the unifying principles of the living state.
- We theorize the unifying principle underlying the stability of gels by means of quantum field theory (QFT).
- Hence, there is good reason to believe that QFT is at least necessary for the understanding of life.
- On the other hand, given that life works against free-energy gradients, QFT in its present form cannot provide a sufficient explanation of life.
- The full understanding of life—especially an understanding of how normative agency can arise out of mere quantum coherence—will most likely require some modification of QFT (such as new conservation principles specific to the living state).

With these points in mind, we can begin to get at least a glimpse of how the philosophical arguments for the material constitution principle might be cashed out in terms of empirical science.

To be sure, the above considerations remain highly speculative. Whether the full story lies in a modification of QFT alone seems doubtful.[19] What seems certain, though, is this: If we are ever to get past Darwinism and oppose scientism successfully, then we must attempt to understand, at least in principle, what an organism might be, if it is not a machine. For, no effective refutation of scientism is conceivable until we have put Darwin into our rear-view mirror, once and for all.

---

[18] Hueschen & Phillips (2024); for discussion, see Barham (forthcoming).

[19] One serious proposal is the "theory of the organism" advanced by Giuseppe Longo, Alvaro Moreno, and their associates across several books (e.g., Longo & Montévil, 2014; Moreno & Mossio, 2015) and a programmatic set of papers (Soto et al., 2016a; Mossio et al., 2016; Montévil et al., 2016; and Soto et al., 2016b). Other provocative approaches to the foundations of life have been advanced by Jonas (1966), Noble (2017), Rosen (1991), E. Thompson (2007), and Yates (1994), among others. However, it seems to me that none of the ideas contained in these works provides us with the ultimate key to the problem.

6. Sentient Agency

6.1. Sentience as a Form of Life

This chapter provides a conceptual bridge between natural, or vital, agency[1] and the uniquely human forms of agency we are calling "intellect" and "spirit." Less abstractly, it investigates some of the specific ways in which the latter phenomena are continuous with the animal form of mind—which I will refer to as "sentience"—and the ways in which they are sharply discontinuous with it. Since no philosophy of nature which neglects or downplays either the continuity or the discontinuity can hope to stand, we must attempt to reconcile them as best we can.

One of the most important foundation stones supporting the scientistic worldview has traditionally been what one might call "neural reductionism." I take this to be, roughly, the idea that thinking, feeling, willing, and acting can all be "reduced" to the level of the activity of the individual neurons, especially to the release of neurotransmitters and the firing of electrical impulses across the synapses. I will address this widespread but mistaken belief in this chapter. Another closely related, spurious claim to the effect that the brain is literally a kind of "computer" will be touched upon in this chapter, as well. (Note that the idea that the brain is a computer is the essential tenet of the fashionable doctrine known as "computationalism.") However, closer examination of the principal reason—having to do with the nature of symbolic representation—that I will adduce in opposition to computationalism will be postponed until the following chapter.

---

[1] From this point forward, I will take the two terms to be equivalent and will use them interchangeably.

My chief inspiration for a positive, organizing viewpoint on the brain will be drawn from Aristotle's model of the tripartite *psukhē* ("soul," or better, "animating principle"). It is reassuring that his model conforms to enlightened common sense in many respects. One of my main goals in the middle chapters of this book is to show how it also comports with the findings of the present-day natural sciences, properly construed.

The traditional Aristotelian model of the human soul posits a three-way distinction between (1) a *threptikē psukhē* ["nutritive soul"] in all life forms,[2] (2) *aisthēsis* ["feeling" or "perception"]— also called an *aisthētikē arkhē* ["sensitive principle"]—in animals,[3] and (3) a *dianoētikē psukhē* ["rational soul"] in human beings.[4] It is perhaps worth noting that at least one ancient Chinese author— the philosopher Xunzi (c. 310–after 238 BC)[5]—concurs with this scheme:[6]

> Fire and water possess energy but are without life. Grass and trees have life but no intelligence. Birds and beasts have intelligence but no sense of duty. Man possesses energy, life, intelligence, and, in addition, a sense of duty. Therefore he is the noblest being on earth.

The first of the three forms of the animating principle, or *psukhē*— which is life as such—was already touched upon above. Translating the second and third forms of *psukhē* into contemporary scientific and philosophical terms, then, will be a primary focus of this chapter and the next.

---

[2] *De Anima*, II.4, 415^{a}14–415^{b}27; and III.12, 434^{a}22–29; Aristotle (1993: 17–19, 72–73).

[3] *De Anima*, III.12, 434^{a}30–434^{b}8; Aristotle (1993: 72–73), and "On Youth and Old Age. On Life and Death," II, 468^{b}4; Aristotle (1936: 417), respectively.

[4] *De Anima*, III.7, 431^{a}14–17; Aristotle (1993: 63). Other terms Aristotle uses in the *De Anima* to designate the distinctively human part of the animating principle (*psukhē*) include *logismos* ["reasoning"] and *dianoia* ["understanding"], both at II.3, 415^{a}8; Aristotle (1993; 16), and, above all, *nous* ["intellect"], at II.3, 414^{b}19, and III.4, 429^{a}22–23; Aristotle (1993; 15, 57), and elsewhere. For discussion, see Johansen (2012).

[5] Thus, Xunzi was born not long after the death of Aristotle.

[6] *Xunzi*, Knoblock 9.16a (II.103) (Watson, 2003: 47).

One aspect of the discussion in this chapter will simply consist in conceptual clarification. However, I will also review some details of brain anatomy, touching briefly upon some of the technological means by which they are obtained. The goal of this review will be to gain some insight into which of the various theories of brain functioning currently on offer comports best with the empirical evidence at our disposal. I will introduce these matters more in order to show how the conception of natural agency might be extended to multicellular organisms with brains—*i.e.*, the higher animals—than for their own sake. My conclusion will probably come as no surprise:

> As the principal locus of centralized control of a multicellular body in the higher animals, the brain is best viewed as a novel, emergent, natural agent in its own right.

Here is how I plan on structuring this chapter. First, I will discuss the relation between consciousness and agency, which I will maintain are distinct facets of sentience that are too often run together. Next, I will introduce the neuroscientific basis for my view of sentience as natural agency. Finally, I will examine some aspects of the evolutionary history of animals that seem germane to the problem of the nature and origin of sentient agency.

6.2. Consciousness and Agency

I would like to begin by explaining more fully what I mean by "consciousness." When employing this term, I have in mind the so-called "hard problem" of consciousness mentioned above. This unique and mysterious state of being is referred to by various terms and phrases, including "subjectivity," "feeling," "phenomenal experience," "interiority," and "what it's like to be" a certain sort of living creature, to mention a few of the favorites. It is intuitively obvious that this state occurs in (at least) the "higher animals," by which I mean chiefly the highly encephalized vertebrates.[7] This intuition rests first and foremost on my interactions with, let's say, my dog Marty, which convince me that "there is someone at home there" in just the same

---

[7] There are, of course, a few outliers among the invertebrates, especially the cephalopods.

way that my interactions with other human beings convince me they are like myself in this respect.[8]

In addition to my straightforward sense that Marty has an interior life of his own, there are also more "scientific" considerations. First and foremost, we know that canine and human brain anatomy are quite similar—and, of course, we know on independent grounds that our own interiority depends upon our brains in a host of ways. Finally, if Marty required a serious operation, he would receive an anesthetic from the veterinarian in just the same way that I would from the anesthesiologist. So, my "phenomenological sympathy" with Marty (as we may call it), his brain anatomy, and the way that anesthetic drugs work on him all converge on the judgment that he enjoys an interior life in the same way that I do. The *nature* of that interior life is another story, of course. Marty's phenomenal experience or interiority is no doubt qualitatively different from mine in a host of ways. The sources and the nature of this difference will be the principal subject of chapter 7. But for the present, I will focus on the similarities between Marty and me—that is, between all higher animals and all human beings—with respect to interiority, or consciousness.

Now, the hard problem asks: How can we bridge the explanatory gap between the so-called "neural correlates of consciousness" (NCCs)—*i.e.*, the anatomical structures of the brain associated with consciousness as demonstrated by the effects of general anesthesia—and the existence of the interior states that Marty and I both enjoy? To this question, I am afraid that I have nothing useful to say. Neither does anyone else, so far as I am aware.[9] The natural phenomenon of consciousness remains an utter mystery, far beyond our ken at present, if not forever.

Why do I say this? Because, while knowledge of the details of brain anatomy and functioning is all well and good, knowing the "wiring diagram" linking the olfactory cortex to the hippocampus,

---

[8] Always remembering that for present purposes we have agreed to set aside general skepticism, which obviously includes skepticism about other minds.

[9] For a refreshing acknowledgment by a neuroscientist and a cognitive psychologist that identifying the NCCs will do little or nothing to solve the hard problem, see Overgaard & Mogensen (2021).

for example, will never suffice in and of itself to explain the quality of Marcel's shattering experience upon tasting the *petite madeleine* in Proust's *In Search of Lost Time*.[10]

That is why I will *not* be pursuing here the traditional strategy of focusing on consciousness. The reason is simply that it would be pointless. Rather, I will be looking at matters from the other way around. That is, instead of enlisting the NCCs in the hopeless task of trying to explain consciousness, I propose to use them to help explain the form that natural agency takes in the higher animals. In so doing, I will be in effect distinguishing between consciousness—often referred to in the anethesthesiology literature as "wakeful aware-ness"—and natural agency as (at least) formally distinct aspects of "sentience." Admittedly, I cannot point to ordinary linguistic usage to justify this move, seeing that the word "sentience" is systematically ambiguous with respect to animal consciousness and agency. On the other hand, I submit that the distinction is intuitively clear. What is more, I believe it can be shown empirically that it is not merely a formal distinction, but a real one. If that is so, then it is incumbent upon us to attempt to bring the distinction to wider attention before its neglect has any further adverse consequences beyond the consid-erable confusion in the philosophical literature it has already sown.

How can the legitimacy of the distinction between sentient consciousness and agency be demonstrated? First, notice that it is possible to suppress all capacity for goal-directed motor activity without completely suppressing wakeful awareness. The anesthesi-ology literature refers to this as the so-called "disconnected" state, meaning that the subject is aware of its surroundings without being able to interact with them.[11] Interestingly, the converse relation does not hold: It is impossible, for all practical purposes, to suppress wakeful awareness without also suppressing the capacity for goal-

---

[10] *À la recherche du temps perdu;* Volume I: *Swann's Way* (*Du côté de chez Swann*); "Part One: Combrai"; near the end of section I; Proust (2003: I, 60).

[11] See Sanders *et al.* (2012). This "disconnected" form of wakeful awareness in animals would appear to be equivalent to "locked-in syndrome" and similar paralytic states in humans.

directed motor activity.[12] Therefore, it would seem we are safe in saying that in higher animals sentience *qua* the exercise of natural agency causally depends upon sentience *qua* wakeful awareness, but not the other way around. And this is enough (1) to warrant a real distinction between wakeful awareness (consciousness) and agency and, nevertheless, (2) to justify our making use of information about consciousness gleaned from the literature on the NCCs to investigate sentient agency.[13] The same considerations also justify our intentional neglect of the hard problem of consciousness.[14]

6.3. The Neuroscience of Sentient Agency

What do we really *know* about the relation between sentience *qua* consciousness and brains? Both a lot and not very much.

For example, we know that, in animals as in humans, general anesthetics target a large number of neural and other cell receptors in various, widely separated regions of the brain—notably, the thalamus and the cerebral cortex. Many researchers interpret this far-flung dispersal of the NCCs to mean that human consciousness is correlated with the "binding" of electrical activity arising from many different parts of the brain. As one team of distinguished investigators has put it:[15]

> Abundant evidence suggests that synchronization within and among these regions may play a critical role in integrating such dispersed information into a unified perception. Cognitive binding

---

[12] Sleepwalking and similar states do not count as cases of the complete suppression of wakeful awareness (unconsciousness); rather, they represent a state of only partial disconnectedness.

[13] I table here the fascinating question of how far down the natural hierarchy sentience *qua* consciousness extends—in other words, just how primitive a nervous system may be and still provide the necessary physical basis for interiority. On this question, see, especially, Ginsburg & Jablonka (2019).

[14] Those familiar with the literature might be tempted to say I treat animals in chapter 6 as "philosophical zombies." Fair enough. However, it does not follow that I regard them as Cartesian automata. On the contrary.

[15] John & Prichep (2005: 450). For discussion focused on the binding issue, see Engel & Fries (2015), Engel & Singer (2001), John (2005), and Mashour (2004, 2013, 2015). For discussion of the NCCs more generally, see Alkire & Miller (2005), Alkire *et al.* (2008), and Bonhomme *et al.* (2019).

at all levels plays a crucial role in the generation of conscious experience.

Taking this type of evidence, then, as also throwing light on the nature of sentience *qua* agency, we are entitled to infer a similar binding of widely dispersed neural activity in the latter case, as well. This binding, in turn, suggests the existence of a *unifying principle* underlying the embodiment of sentient agency in brains.

All this may appear to provide us with quite a bit of knowledge about how brains produce agency. However, viewed from a different angle, it does not really tell us very much about what we most wish to know. Specifically, it tells us only that the binding of widely dispersed neural activity occurs somehow or other, not how it is *possible* for it to occur. That is, while knowledge of the NCCs points to the *existence* of a unifying principle binding neural activity into a single, unified capacity for acting, it does little in and of itself to *characterize* that principle, much less *explain* it.

Of course, neuroscience relies upon much more than just the NCCs to provide it with the empirical foundation for its theoretical models of brain functioning. Much of the genuine, if modest, progress in the study of the brain in recent years has come about thanks to improved brain-imaging techniques, especially real-time "functional magnetic resonance imaging" (fMRI), which measures the differential metabolic activity of diverse brain regions as a proxy for neural functional activity.[16] Together with older forms of monitoring the brain's electrical activity, such electroencephalography (EEG), the patch clamp technique, and others, fMRI technology has certainly contributed much useful and theoretically suggestive knowledge over the past several decades about the relation between the brain's anatomical structure and its functioning.

---

[16] While this assumed equivalence is entirely reasonable, we should not allow ourselves to get carried away by the considerable hype surrounding fMRI or forget how crude a technique it really is. Investigating brain functioning by means of fMRI is like attempting to explain how a computer works by measuring the temperature of its parts. Not unreasonable, perhaps, in its own way, but a very blunt instrument indeed. For an authoritative and measured discussion of fMRI technology, see Shulman (2013).

Of course, different neuroscientists have tended to interpret the body of empirical knowledge gathered by these various technologies in different ways. That is only to be expected and, in any case, it is of course not up to philosophers to dictate to scientists. But what I am permitted to do in the present context *qua* philosopher is to survey the various theoretical interpretations of the agreed-upon facts that are on offer, in order to see if any of them may be of special interest to proponents of reformed naturalism, of the Aristotelian tripartite animating principle, of vital agency, of emergence, and of freedom.

I believe that one school of neuroscientific theory stands out as being of particular interest to us in these respects. I am thinking of the attempts to model brain functioning by means of the field of mathematics that have come to be known as "dynamical systems theory."[17] On this view, brain functioning is the result of the integration of the activity of widely dispersed groups of neurons (called "nerve cell assemblies"), which fire in synchrony. Thus, there is coordination of electrical activity on multiple levels simultaneously. On this view—assuming electrical activity is a proxy for functional activity—the brain's resting state is regarded as akin to the ground state of a "field," while individual acts of perceiving, thinking, willing, and so on are analogous to higher-level "virtual states" that regions of the field may assume. Recall, too, that this conclusion deriving from cognitive neuroscience also coheres with the evidence from general anesthesia, which points to the large-scale "binding" of neural activity dispersed throughout the cerebral cortex and the brain stem.

I submit that the findings from investigations into the NCCs, data from fMRI, EEG, and other technological probes, and the school of theoretical neuroscience which models brain functioning by means of dynamical systems theory all point in the same direction. According to contemporary neuroscience, far from being reducible to the firing of the synapses, the brain's functional activity may be more properly

---

[17] See, especially, the work of Walter J. Freeman and his colleagues on the integration of perception and action: e.g., Freeman (2001), Freeman & Vitiello (2006), Kozma & Freeman (2019), and Skarda & Freeman (1987). See, also, Başar (2004), Buzsáki (2006), Raichle (2010, 2015), and Yuste *et al.* (2005). For a similar perspective on the integration of affect, see LaRock *et al.* (2020).

viewed as arising out of the capacities of the brain as a new kind of emergent natural agent in its own right.

6.4. The Evolution of Sentient Agency

Needless to say, the above considerations are still not decisive. Therefore, let us step back for a moment and attempt to open up a new line of attack on our problem by looking at it from a wider perspective. Specifically, let us ask ourselves the question: What is the *purpose* of central nervous systems and brains?

First, it should be noted that the roots of multicellularity run very deep in the foundations of life, being already present in bacteria and similar single-celled, prokaryotic organisms in the form of the capacity of individual cells to congregate into social groups.[18] For such coordination of the actions of individual cells to be possible, they must engage in some sort of "communication," "signaling," or "information exchange" with one another.[19]

Second, in addition to this primordial form of sociality found among the bacteria, a somewhat different form of sociality is found among the single-celled, eukaryotic organisms known as "slime molds" (a kind of amoeba). At the reproductive stage of their life cycle, these creatures come together to form organism-like "fruiting bodies." These fruiting bodies are capable of moving collectively in a coherent manner reminiscent of an animal. Afterwards, the individual cells that make up a fruiting body disaggregate and resume their previous life of foraging as individual cells.[20]

Third, there are what we might call the "dedicated" multicellular organisms—life forms which grow from a single cell into a perma-

---

[18] See Hagen (2017), Monds & O'Toole (2008), Shapiro & Dworkin (1997), and von Bodman *et al.* (2008).

[19] However, a *caveat* must be registered here: One must employ the word "information" with some care. It is widely used in an undiscriminating manner, which equivocates between technical syntactic and commonsense semantic senses of the term. This practice has had the unfortunate result of introducing great confusion into the literature. I cannot discuss this issue in detail in this Introduction, but I will address it briefly later in this chapter. See, also, Barham (1996) and Withagen & van der Kamp (2010).

[20] See Bonner (2009).

nent, more or less tightly integrated grouping of cells, thus remaining "social" creatures, as it were, throughout their life cycle. I have in mind here, of course, principally the plants and the animals.

In the case of bacteria, slime-mold fruiting bodies, and plants, the various forms of sociality they achieve are brought about exclusively through *chemical* means. So, chemical signaling appears to be an element of vital agency as such. To all appearances, there is no single component part of a cell—or of a slime-mold fruiting body or of a plant—which controls the whole system.[21] That is, none of the organisms that unite socially by chemical means have brains or indeed any kind of nervous tissue at all.

With the animals, we come to a very different basis for the coordination of the multicellular condition. Many marine invertebrates, including sponges, sea anemones, flatworms, sea slugs, starfish, and others, do not have central nervous systems or brains as such, but do possess *nerve nets*. In some of the above-mentioned animals, there is also a specialized region of the nerve net called the *ganglion*, which is a small clump of neurons that may be regarded as a protobrain. Nerve nets (with and without ganglia) make it possible for these animals to pursue an entirely different way of life from that of plants and single-celled organisms. This is, of course, even truer of the higher animals possessing true central nervous systems with well-developed brains.[22] In the latter case, it is clear that the brain exercises a high degree of centralized control over the multicellular organism as a whole.[23]

But why do such animals exist in the first place? What are brains *for*, exactly?

Ordinarily, to answer questions of this sort biologists recur to the theory of natural selection, invoking some respect in which the novel trait to be explained is functionally superior, which then leads

---

[21] For the contrary view that the centrosome may serve as a sort of "brain" in individual cells, see Albrecht-Buehler (2013).

[22] See Arnellos & Moreno (2016), Macphail (1993), and Niklas & Dunker (2016).

[23] While only a small portion of this control is conscious, much of it occurring below the level of wakeful awareness by means of the autonomic nervous system, I ignore this complication for ease of exposition.

to differential reproduction and the gradual spreading of the trait throughout the population. However, as we have already seen, this approach begs the question of the source of agency by simply *assuming* the existence of the functionally superior trait. In other words, the Darwinian schema gets the causation backwards. It is the existence of sociality, multicellularity, and brains that we are asking about. Merely to *assume* the existence of these phenomena in order to "explain" the differential reproduction of the organisms which possess them would throw no light at all on the questions that concern us.

Granted, alternative explanatory frameworks for the origin of functional traits in organisms are not exactly thick on the ground. However, one promising perspective that has come to the fore in recent decades at least gets the causation the right way around. I am thinking of the so-called "theory of self-organization."[24]

I must pause here to mention that it is imperative to distinguish the notion of "self-organization" from the concept of "self-ordering" with which it is sometimes confused. Properly speaking, "self-organization" applies only to the actions of vital agents considered as organized wholes. "Self-ordering," in contrast, is a process which occurs mostly in many-body, inorganic systems, such as Bénard cells, the Belousov-Zhabotinsky reaction, hurricanes, and so forth, although it may also occur in certain physical processes taking place within cells, as well, such as the spontaneous self-assembly of a bilayer lipid membrane out its component molecular parts. Self-ordering phenomena are relatively well understood, the relevant explanatory theory deriving from the discipline of nonequilibrium thermodynamics. However, all such phenomena ultimately result from free-energy minimization and, as we saw above, the holistic action of a vital agent cannot be explained in such terms. This does not mean that the principles of non-equilibrium thermodynamics have no potential relevance to self-organization. It just means that we

---

[24] Also known by the terms "complex systems theory," "spontaneous order," and other appellations. See Bar-Yam (2019), Camazine *et al.* (2001), Kauffman (1993), and Satz (2020). This disparate field of research is largely based on concepts borrowed from the discipline of nonequilibrium thermodynamics. See Kondepudi & Prigogine (2014).

must be very cautious in our attempts to understand self-organization in terms of principles that are primarily applicable to self-ordering.

For this reason, in the absence of a well-developed theory of self-organization, our best recourse may well be simply to go on talking about the phenomena of primary interest to us in functional terms. Such a discourse will resemble that of the traditional Darwinian evolutionary biologist, with this major difference: Our goal will be *not* to reduce the agential (teleological, evaluative, normative) properties of organisms to mechanical interactions, but rather to show how a living thing with a certain set of agential characteristics, existing at a given hierarchical level, may be understood as having emerged out of a historically prior kind of agent existing at a lower hierarchical level. In this way, we may hope to be able to fill in what would otherwise be a substantial gap in our picture of the evolution of the higher forms of agency and freedom.

The reason why the condition of multicellularity poses a special problem for animals, requiring a special solution, is that animals move in a coordinated way through space. Why is this a problem? Remember that every living cell of an animal's body is a vital agent with a life and interests of its own. For an organism to be able to adopt the animal way of life, all these myriad vital agents must somehow be cajoled into moving through space together as a corporate whole. After all, the well-being of each of them depends upon the well-being of the whole animal to which they belong. For this reason, we are on safe ground in concluding that the primary purpose of brains is to make possible the coherent motion of multicellular animal bodies through space.

This idea has two additional implications. First, the individual cells that make up multicellular animals must undergo a stronger form of subjugation to the common good, so to speak, than is the case with bacteria, slime-mold fruiting bodies, or plants. Second, because the chemical signals that the latter entities depend upon to achieve sociality travel relatively slowly, a faster kind of signaling is required for animals, which typically move through space far more rapidly than chemicals diffuse. Nervous systems with brains fulfill both these conditions: (1) They unite the component parts of animal bodies by imposing centralized control upon them; and (2) The electrical signals they utilize to achieve this control travel much more swiftly than chemical signals, enabling rapid adjustments to be made to the whole animal's movements through space.

In short, the evolutionary history of animals coheres with the empirical evidence from neuroscience. This permits us to conclude that an animal's brain stands in the same relation to the rest of its body's component parts, down to the level of individual cells, that the principle of vital agency that unifies a single cell (whatever it may turn out to be) stands in relation to the cell's macromolecules, organelles, and so on.

* * *

Finally, here are some additional issues that would have to be addressed in a truly comprehensive investigation, presented in summary fashion:

- Viewing the brain as a coherent dynamical system and a natural agent obviates the need for us to think of it as a computer;[25]
- The dynamical-systems/natural-agent model of the brain also allows us to dispense with the question-begging concept of "representation."[26] On the present view, the term "representation" ought to be used only in reference to arbitrary (conventional) "symbols." Representation in this sense first arises in connection with human language.
- There is, however, a legitimate sense in which all vital agents as such employ "signals" ("communicate"). Whence the need to examine the concept of "biosemiosis," which is based not upon symbolic representations, but upon "natural signs."[27]

---

[25] See van Gelder (1995). For more-recent discussions of this perspective, see di Paolo, et al. (2017), Hutto *et al.* (2018), and Stewart, et al. (2010).

[26] There is a vast literature on dynamical-systems, non-representationalist approaches to cognitive science, for which the following will have to stand proxy here: Chemero (2009), Juarrero (1999), Hanna & Maiese (2009), Kiverstein & Rietveld (2018, 2021), Newen *et al.* (2018), Noble & Noble (2021), and Zahnoun (2020, 2021a, 2021b).

- The dynamical systems/natural agent model of the brain also coheres nicely with work done in the field of ecological psychology on the physiological construction of "perception-action cycles."[28]
- Finally, identifying the natural agent that constitutes the unifying principle of the animal body with the brain's "field" of coherent and coordinated electrical activity suggests a new version of the old "identity" position within the literature on the mind/body problem: "non-reductionist (or emergentist) identity theory."[29]

To sum up this chapter: If we are to successfully oppose scientism, it is important that we get our human nature right. This means, above all, avoiding the twin perils of demeaning human beings into "just another animal," on the one hand, and of vaulting us into a transcendent realm beyond this world, on the other. That is why a clear-eyed outlook on animal sentience—both how it is continuous and how it is discontinuous with the human intellect and spirit—is absolutely crucial to striking the correct balance regarding our place in nature. In this chapter, I have outlined the argument for continuity between

---

[27] See, *e.g.*, Barbieri (2006, 2013), Emmeche & Kull (2011), Favareau (2010), and Hoffmeyer (2008).

[28] See the work of James J. Gibson and others associated with the "ecological psychology" movement: *e.g.*, Gibson (1977, 1979), Kugler & Turvey (1987), Turvey (2019), and Wagman & Blau (2019). For criticism of the way Gibson's notion of "affordance" has been misused within the mainstream (representationalist) cognitive science literature, see Chong & Proctor (2020). It must be admitted that Gibson and his colleagues have invited this confusion by continuing to employ the term "information" in their writings in an uncritical fashion. Nonetheless, I maintain that ecological psychology—if coupled with the dynamical-systems approach to brain function—is in fact perfectly compatible with a non-representationalist understanding of perception and action, at least in nonhuman animals and in human action contexts sufficiently remote from linguistically mediated conceptual categorization. On the further question of the compatibility between ecological-psychology and dynamical-systems approaches to perception and action, see Read & Szokolszky (2020).

[29] For an excellent discussion (albeit from a somewhat different perspective), see Myin & Zahnoun (2018). It must always be kept in mind that we are talking about the nature of the *agent* constituted by the brain's coherent electrical activity. Simply moving from the level of synapses to the level of fields and the whole brain does not advance us a single step towards a solution to the hard problem of consciousness.

sentient and rational agency. For the discontinuity, let us now turn to the next chapter.

7. Rational Agency and the Human Spirit

Thus Thought composes, above the physical world, a moral, a social, a human, an aesthetical, a religious world, which, although not reducible to material elements, is nevertheless real, and worthy of subsisting and developing.

—Émile Boutroux (1918: 22)

7.1. The Human Spirit as World 3

In some ways, this chapter is the most challenging one in this book. Certainly, it is one in which it is of the utmost importance to strike a delicate balance between two extreme views—both of which are more popular than the intermediate one on offer here—if we are to have any hope of effectively combatting scientism. The question was well-posed by the Psalmist:[1]

What is man, that thou art mindful of him? and the son of man, that thou visitest him?
For thou hast made him a little lower than the angels, and hast crowned him with glory and honour.

In short, how can we say what it is that makes us so different from the other animals, without untethering ourselves from the animal kingdom, and with it the physical world, altogether? For we manifestly *are* animals and we *do* live in the physical world.

---

[1] Psalms, 8:4–5 (KJV).

By now it will be clear that I hold the answer to be that human beings inhabit a special domain of reality I have been calling "spirit." I have already tried to demonstrate what I have in mind by "spirit" above, with the aid of a little "thought experiment" designed to dramatize the way we human beings inhabit an intellectual and emotional world that is utterly beyond the ken of the other animals. I call this domain of reality "intellect," insofar as it manifests in each individual human being, and "spirit," when all the intellects are taken collectively. Whereas intellect is intimately connected to consciousness, and to this extent is a subjective or "psychological" phenomenon, spirit has an altogether different ontological foundation that is entirely objective (non-subjective, non-psychological) in character.

For this reason, the account developed here may be seen as a further contribution to the continuing struggle against "psychologism"—the doctrine dating back to nineteenth-century German materialism, which would have it that thoughts are reducible to the physical goings-on in brains. On the other hand, I do not want to settle for a dualistic or "Platonistic" picture of the relation between thinking and its material substrate, either. The emergentist picture being drawn in this book aims at finding a middle way between psychologism and Platonism.

The term "spirit" lends itself to this project for several reasons. One is, as I mentioned above, the reductionist (psychologistic) connotation of the term "mind" in current philosophical discourse. Another reason is that "mind" is too individualistic, whereas "spirit" more properly expresses the essentially collective or social dimension of the domain of reality under discussion. Lastly, the term "spirit" conforms much better with the decisive distinction that must be drawn between the *sui generis* human world as such—which has an objective existence apart from any concrete human intellect—and the subjective or "psychological" state of being that is shared by individual human beings with the higher animals, as discussed in the previous chapter.

I also borrow the term "spirit" because, as discussed above, it seems to me to be the best translation of the German term *Geist*. I mention this in order to highlight the kinship between my conception of the human spirit and such ideas as Gottlob Frege's concept of a *drittes Reich* ["third realm"][2] and Karl Popper's notion of a "World 3."[3] These thinkers introduced these concepts precisely in order to distinguish the realm of objective truth and knowledge from the psychological goings-on within concrete human individuals. Aristotle, too, had a similar, if dark, doctrine of what he called the *"nous poiētikos"* [standardly translated as "active intellect"], which seems to be something shared in common by all finite human intellects.[4] Unfortunately, none of these authors says very much about the ontological status of this separate, objectively existing domain of intellectual reality.

For our part, we must clarify, above all, how it is possible for spirit to be *both* ontologically grounded in finite intellects—where it constitutes a new form of sentience exerting centralized control over a multicellular animal body—*and* emergent from such intellects, constituting another novel level of reality in its own right. Let us begin this daunting task by making some more homely observations about the powers and capacities possessed by all human beings and only human beings.

As a first stab in this direction, recall the last stanza of Robert Burns's magnificent apostrophe to a mouse whose nest he had turned up with his plow:[5]

> Still, thou art blest, compar'd wi' *me*!
> The *present* only toucheth thee:
> But Och! I *backward* cast my e'e,
> On prospects drear!

---

[2] Frege (1997).

[3] Popper (1972). For discussion of the three-worlds ontology, see Radovan (2024).

[4] *De Anima*, III.4–5, 429ᵃ10–430ᵃ25; Aristotle (1993: 57–60). For discussion, see Burnyeat (2008). For the late-Antique tradition regarding the "active intellect," see Schroeder (2014) and Schroeder & Todd (1990). For the medieval-Islamic tradition, see Davidson (1992).

[5] "To a Mouse, On turning her up in her Nest, with the Plough, November, 1785"; Burns (1993: 68).

An' *forward,* tho' I canna *see,*
I *guess* an' *fear!*
   (original emphasis)

We may refer to the human capacity invoked here by the poet as "imagination."[6] It is arguably one of the most important pieces of the puzzle of the human difference. As Burns indicates, it appears to be directly linked to our ability to think about states of affairs that are remote from us in space (non-local) and in time (non-present). Moreover, it is imagination that allows us to think about general, counterfactual, fictional, and other kinds of intellectual constructs and scenarios. Finally, imagination provides us with the all-important capacity to take up other points of view on reality than our own.

At first sight, imagination may appear to be a distinctively *cognitive* power—which is indeed more or less what we are looking for. However, this observation requires immediate qualification. It would, in fact, be a serious mistake to look upon the human difference as *only* cognitive, or intellectual. Rather, the power of the human imagination lies at the center of our affective lives, as well, which are also of an entirely different metaphysical order from the emotional lives of the other animals.

How can I make such a sweeping claim with such confidence? A thousand examples spring to mind, but here is one of my favorites. It has been observed that when a newborn chimpanzee dies, its mother may carry her baby's dead body around with her for many days. After several days or, at most, weeks, however, she will simply toss the body away.[7] Compare this to the human situation as illustrated, for example, by the scene from Robert Bresson's great film version[8] of Georges Bernanos's novel, *Diary of a Country Priest,*[9] in which

---

[6] Aristotle concurs—see his discussion of *phantasia* at *De Anima,* III.11, 433^{b}31–434^{a}15; Aristotle (1993: 71–72). See, also, Wedin (1988). For more general philosophical reflection upon imagination, see Bogdan (2013), Brann (1993), and Warnock (1976). Though Bogdan is strangely dismissive of language and generally prey to scientism, he nevertheless provides the most useful philosophical analysis of the link between intellect and imagination.

[7] See, e.g., Goodall (1971). For a more recent report, see Biro (2010).

[8] *Journal d'un curé de campagne* [Diary of a Country Priest] (1951).

[9] Bernanos (1937).

the young priest of Ambricourt struggles with the Countess over a locket containing a photograph of her dead son, which she has worn upon her person and cherished for decades. Indeed, she has lived in seclusion during all these years, and will die later that same night, all as a result of her unassuageable grief for the boy.

To be sure, the human mother's capacity for experiencing grief doubtless rests, in part, on maternal instincts she shares with the chimpanzee mother. Still, the difference between the chimpanzee's reaction to the death of her infant and the human being's reaction to the kind sort of loss could hardly be starker—a grief of a few days' duration compared to one that is unbounded in time.

That, in a nutshell, is the human difference. It is also unforgettably expressed by Shakespeare's King Claudius:[10]

> [P]oor Ophelia
>> Divided from herself and her fair judgment,
>> Without the which we are pictures, or mere beasts

Clearly, it is not unrelated to the *cognitive* faculty of imagination. But it is vitally important to keep in mind how imagination permeates, not just our intellects, but also our emotional lives and indeed the whole of our lived experience.

Armed with these observations, let us now return to the main task at hand: that of conceiving how spirit can be both ontologically grounded in concrete, individual human intellects and quasi-independent from them in such a way as to create a new, superior level of reality. It will come as little surprise to readers to learn that I concur with nearly all authors who comment on this topic that the answer lies in the human faculty of *language*. For, as Aristotle famously noted:[11]

> [M]an alone among the animals possesses speech.

Hegel concurs with Aristotle, and expands significantly upon the theme:[12]

---

[10] *Hamlet*, Act IV, Scene V.

[11] *logon de monon anthrōpos ekhei tōn zōiōn*, *Politics*, I.1, 1253ª10–11; Aristotle (1995: 3).

[12] *Wissenschaft der Logik*, Volume One, Book One, "Preface to the First Edition" (1812); Hegel (2010: 12).

> The forms of thought are first set out and stored in human *language,* and one can hardly be reminded often enough nowadays that thought is what differentiates the human being from the beast. In everything that the human being has interiorized, in everything that in some way or other has become for him a representation, in whatever he has made his own, there has language penetrated. (original emphasis)

But these observations, which have become commonplace, immediately give rise to two further questions that must be carefully distinguished:

1. How, precisely, does language give rise to spirit?
2. How did language itself come into being in the first place?

7.2. Spirit and Language

Taking the second question first, in all the vast and inconclusive literature on the origin of language, the most promising proposal I have seen is that of Denis Bouchard.[13] He has presented suggestive empirical evidence for the existence of what he calls "offline brain systems." In terms of the vocabulary we have developed here, these would be natural agents (or subagents) embodied in the brain's field-like unifying principle, which are not directly coupled to the environment, but instead are able to monitor the activity of the brain itself—i.e., that of other neural subagents. Such offline brain systems, if they are confirmed to exist, would go a long way towards explaining our capacity to inhibit (and also excite) our own spontaneously initiated behavior on the basis of higher-level constraints emanating from the domain of spirit (promises, values, ideals, etc.)—which, I submit, is as good a description as any of "free will."

Such a view also accords well with the understanding of "conscience" as a second-order, rational restraint, or "inner check," upon our spontaneous, first-order inclinations. In the words of Bishop

---

[13] Bouchard (2013; 2021).

Butler:[14]

> There is a principle of reflection in men, by which they distinguish between, approve and disapprove their own actions. We are plainly constituted such sort of creatures as to reflect upon our own nature. The mind can take a view of what passes within itself, its propensities, aversions, passions, affections, as respecting such objects, and in such degrees; and of the several actions consequent thereupon. . . . This principle in man, by which he approves or disapproves his heart, temper, and actions, is conscience . . .

The foregoing considerations provide the basis for the following propositions:

- The human difference lies in intellect and spirit.
- Spirit is ontologically grounded in language.
- Thus, language is the main force that transformed sentient agency into rational agency.

Now, the skeptical reader will rightly have many questions about these propositions. Perhaps the most important one will relate to the admittedly enormous gap between the mere existence of offline brain systems and symbol-based language use. Bouchard has argued that nothing more than the former is required for the association of mental categories ("concepts") with vocal utterances *qua* arbitrary (conventional) symbols in the form of spoken words, which is one of the main constitutive features of human language.[15] Chomskyites have challenged this idea and it is fair to say that many if not most linguists, philosophers of language, and cognitive scientists continue to insist on the need for "mentalese" (an innate "universal grammar"). But I do not intend to enter into the details of this dispute in this book. Rather, I am content to point to Bouchard's ideas as one plausible model for how a (seemingly) relatively simple modification to brain

---

[14] *Fifteen Sermons Preached at the Rolls Chapel*, Sermon 1: "Upon Human Nature, the Social Nature of Man," §8 (Butler, 2017: 19–20). See, also, Leander (1994).

[15] Other such features include subject-predicate syntax, subordination, recursivity, and other syntactical features. I will discuss the fundamental nature and significance of language further below.

function might provide the foundation for both language and the human form of sociality that language gives rise to.

7.3. The Origin of Spirit

To return to the first question posed above: Once we have a human society using language, we already have *ipso facto* the rudiments of spirit in the shared concepts embodied in the vocabulary of the society's language. With this much, we are *already* in possession of John McDowell's "second nature," at least in a rudimentary form. Now, some might object that other animals, too, have "cultures."[16] What, then, is so special about human culture based on language? To this, I would reply that there is no reason to think the potential for cultural achievements as such—in the sense of behavioral innovations that are handed down from generation to generation through imitation and instruction—must be restricted to humans. But second nature, or spirit, is quite different from animal cultures in two ways: (1) it brings into being, not just a suite of culturally acquired practices, but an entirely new ontological realm of being; and (2) it possesses an open-ended potential for growth from one generation to the next, bringing into being the temporal dimension of human action we call "history. And both of these achievements are based directly upon the innate human capacity for using language.

That said, the main difference between my account of spirit and McDowell's account of second nature is that on my view second nature *already* possesses all the hallmarks of agency—purpose, value, meaning, normativity, and so forth. My model does not attempt to *derive* these phenomena from second nature, but rather properly construes human second nature as an emergent phenomenon arising out of generic biological agency *via* language and imagination.

As such, the reformed naturalist view attempts to blaze a path between "nature" and "nurture" that avoids both the extreme of biological reductionism (unreformed "naturalism," Darwinism, scientism in general) and the extreme of idealism, whether subjective

---

[16] See Avital & Jablonka (2000).

(Kant) or "objective," i.e., social (Hegel, Marx, the myriad forms of postmodern constructivism).

By now, it probably goes without saying that I believe the Aristotelian worldview threads this needle very well. Two key insights flowing from the Aristotelian framework help us to begin to better understand second nature: (1) spirit is an *essential* aspect of human nature, and (2) human nature *qua* biological endowment is *already* teleological and normative.

Aristotle says the following concerning the relation between spirit and our animal nature:[17]

> So virtues arise in us neither by nature nor contrary to nature, but nature gives us the capacity to acquire them, and completion comes through habituation.

This seems to me correct, but it needs elaboration. For that purpose, let me pause for a moment to consider an influential version of the ancient Chinese Ruist ("Confucian") view of moral self-cultivation (*xiushen*) and human nature (*xing*), namely, the teaching of Mengzi (372–289 BC),[18] known in the West since the sixteenth century by the name of "Mencius."

There is much to say about this central issue in Ruist ethics.[19] For our purposes, however, I will focus on a passage from Mencius, which expounds the idea that human nature possesses the biological dispositions (as we might say) that are required for moral self-cultivation.[20]

> From this we can see that if one is without the feeling of compassion, one is not human. If one is without the feeling of disdain, one is not human. If one is without the feeling of deference, one is not human. If one is without the feeling of approval and disapproval, one is not human.

---

[17] *Nicomachean Ethics*, II.1, 1103^{a}24–26; Aristotle (2000: 23).

[18] Note that Mencius's life overlapped with Aristotle's.

[19] For background discussion, see Bloom (1997), Ivanhoe (2000), and Nivison (1996a).

[20] *Mencius*, 2A6.4 (Mencius, 2008: 46). I have omitted the material from traditional commentaries interpolated by the translator.

It is hard to imagine a clearer statement of the species-specific nature of the human moral feelings.

What is even more interesting, though, is that Mencius does not stop there. He does not claim that the moral feelings themselves constitute moral norms, only that they play a necessary role in the process of self-cultivation of a fully formed human moral agent. The feelings must somehow become transformed from subjective states into objective norms if they are to explain the twofold character of human morality. Understanding this, Mencius goes on to specify the relationship between what he sees as our basic, instinctive moral feelings—which he famously terms the "four sprouts" (*siduan*)—and what are for him the four basic virtues:[21]

> The feeling of compassion is the sprout of benevolence. The feeling of disdain is the sprout of righteousness. The feeling of deference is the sprout of propriety. The feeling of approval and disapproval is the sprout of wisdom. People having these four sprouts is like their having four limbs.

In this passage, Mencius links the following crucial concepts:

- The source of moral norms (virtues) is our instinctive moral feelings
- These feelings are a normative feature of human nature, just like our four limbs
- Our four basic moral feelings are transformed into the four virtues through a process of *growth*, by analogy with the way in which sprouts grow into flourishing plants

I submit that Aristotle would have wholeheartedly embraced Mencius's notion of "moral sprouts," had he known of it.

Aristotle and Mencius, then, agree on the basic model I am recommending here. I would merely add that to understand how the human twofold nature is metaphysically possible, it is important to distinguish between the *substrate* of the emergent level—which in this case is the language faculty—and its *content*, which is spirit. Regarding this content, not just entire books, but whole libraries would be required to catalogue the phenomena which constitute and

---

[21] *Mencius*, 2A6.5 (Mencius, 2008: 46–47).

populate it. We will return to this large subject presently. For now, let us look more closely than we have done so far at the metaphysical underpinnings of the content of spirit in the faculties of the individual intellect.

I have already spoken briefly of imagination, noting its connection with the objectivity of spirit. I have also referred to the intellectual constellation consisting of sentience, the language faculty, and imagination as "rational agency." Rational agency is sentient agency under the guidance of imagination and spirit.[22] And imagination is clearly grounded in the language faculty. So far, so good. But more needs to be said on all these points.

In this connection, I wish to introduce another important aspect to the emergence of spirit and with it objectivity—one which relates to the *nature* of language. "Language" is usually taken to be defined by two properties: a set of *arbitrary symbols* ("lexemes") that *refer* to entities of all sorts and a set of permissible *operations* upon those symbols ("grammar") that *connect* the symbols in various ways. The most elementary such operation—known as "predication"—is usually taken to be the attribution of a quality ("predicate") to a substance ("subject"). Thus, we may draw an analogy between *predication* at the level of language and *association* at the level of pre-linguistic cognition. There is something about the nature of language that converts the animal's ability to *act intelligently*, as if by magic, into the human being's ability to *reason*. At least a part of this magic must consist in the power that predication confers upon us to make *assertions*, to judge their *truth-value*, and to make *inferences* on their basis. All of this seems to form a fundamental aspect of *objectivity*, one which gives rise to imagination's power to manipulate the contents of spirit.

Finally, there is a special sense of objectivity which derives from the fact that the content of the domain of spirit *exists* independently of any individual human being (though not of the human race). This sense of objectivity is purely ontological and has nothing to do "intersubjectivity," which is an epistemological concept.

---

[22] Also conscience, but I reserve discussion of that faculty for the next chapter.

What do I mean by the *objectively existing content* of the domain of spirit? I am thinking here of the mode of existence of a vast number of phenomena—often referred to as "intentional objects"—extending from social institutions (kinship systems, governments, laws, money, and so forth), to concrete artifacts (tools, machines, paintings, recitations, performances, and written texts of all kinds), to abstract objects (poems, novels, musical scores, fictional characters, philosophical concepts, scientific theories, and logical and mathematical truths). The late-Scholastic Christian philosophers referred to such contents of spirit, or intentional objects, as *"entia rationis"* [beings of reason].[23] I shall employ this suggestive terminology from time to time.

Beings of reason exist objectively in the sense that their existence does not depend upon any *particular* human intellect, but only on *some* human intellect or other. In other words, while the contents of spirit ontologically depend upon the existence of human intellects, they do so only in a generic way. By ontologically depending upon language, they depend upon the human form of sociality. For language is in large part responsible for the human form of sociality. Or, to speak more precisely, language and the human form of sociality have co-constructed each other.

To sum up, beings of reason are ontologically grounded in the domain of spirit, which is itself grounded in the human language faculty and, with it, the human form of sociality. One may also say that spirit is grounded in language *qua* species trait and not language *qua* individual power or capacity. That is, spirit is grounded in the human species as such.

To round out our view, then, we may say that spirit is an objectively real, albeit *sui generis*, emergent level. It cannot be reduced to the mere operation of the individual human brain (psychologism) any more than it can be detached from matter altogether (Platonism). Also note that instead of reducing human rationality to computation (as "computationalism" would have it), on our view, computers are in fact created by us in the image of spirit. Thus, the position roughed in

---

[23] See Klima (1993) and Novotný (2013, 2019).

here is in some ways the converse of computationalism. Alas, there is no obvious name for it.[24] Perhaps "emergent rationalism" is the least misleading of the various labels that come to mind.

With the articulation of the domain of spirit now in place, the task of this book to provide an alternative worldview to that advanced by the proponents of scientism is nearing completion. However, before finishing, I wish to include two additional chapters, in which I discuss two dimensions of spirit that are particularly salient philosophically: morality and politics.

The reason for these last two chapters is that I believe it is incumbent upon any opponent of scientism to have some idea of how morality and politics fit into the overall program of reformed naturalism. For these two domains of spirit are where scientism has traditionally worked—and is now working—its greatest mischief.

---

[24] "Spiritism" being out of the question for obvious reasons.

8. Human Nature and Morality

8.1. The Specter of Moral Relativism

In this chapter I am concerned with opposing scientism as it manifests itself in the domain of human morality—or just plain "morality," seeing that there is no other kind. This will naturally entail showing, in a constructive way, how morality might be understood as flowing from the nature of a rational agent such as I have been developing in chapter 7—that is, a natural agent possessing intellect and free will, and intimately connected to the emergent domain of spirit.

Some proponents of scientism hold that moral judgments (attributions of moral properties to actions) and the moral properties themselves (right and wrong) have no place in the natural order of things.[1] This doctrine views moral properties as non-existent and their employment as a kind of mistake. This is the so-called "error theory," which is simply a species of eliminationism. Error theory itself may take a variety of forms, including a reductionist form along the lines of Darwinian selection theory.[2] I will return to the Darwinian strategy below.

More common among proponents of scientism than outright moral eliminationism is a different strategy, one which involves accepting that there is a sense in which the terms "right" and "wrong" have legitimate application to actions, but which also claims that the metaphysical ground of this legitimacy lies in pure subjectivity, whether of the individual or of the social group to which he belongs.

---

[1] See Mackie (1977).
[2] See Joyce (2002).

Once again, there are many variations on this theme, which there is no need for us to go into here. What all forms of subjectivism have in common is the basic idea that what makes a moral statement true is something that is nothing objective about the world as it is apart from human subjectivity, but rather something lying in human subjectivity itself, which may vary from person to person or from culture to culture. In short, subjectivism implies *moral relativism*.

Given the importance of moral relativism as a component of the scientistic worldview, and inasmuch as eliminationism and reductionism have already been rejected as general explanatory strategies during the discussion of emergence in chapter 3 above, my discussion in this chapter will be primarily focused on opposing subjectivism in ethics. That is, the ultimate aim of my arguments will be to legitimate the objectivity of right and wrong as properties of actions.

Now, the most common way of arguing for the objectivity of moral values and moral judgments is by attempting to ground them in reason. The idea of either a social contract, or a categorical imperative, or a general utility principle, is alleged to provide us with an understanding of morality such that we can see right (or wrong) actions as logically consistent (or inconsistent) with other things we must accept on pain of contradiction.

However, as David Hume famously observed:[3]

'Tis not contrary to reason to prefer the destruction of the whole world to the scratching of my finger,

Interestingly, another early Chinese philosopher by the name of Yang Zhu (440–c. 360)[4]—who founded the "Yangist" school of philosophical egoism—is reported by Mencius to have said something similar:[5]

Mengzi said, "Yang Zhu favored being 'for oneself.' If plucking out one hair from his body would have benefited the whole world, he would not do it."

---

[3] *A Treatise of Human Nature*, Book II, Part III, Section III (Hume, 1978: 416).

[4] Thus, Yang Zhu (or Yangzi) was a slightly older contemporary of Plato.

[5] *Mencius*, 7A26.1–2 (Mencius, 2008: 178).

In the cited passage, Hume is making a purely conceptual point: When he says it would be "not contrary to reason" to prefer the destruction of the world to a scratch on his finger, he means it would not be *logically inconsistent.* Yang Zhu is saying something slightly different. For the philosophical egoist who wishes to be logically consistent, he ought to prefer the loss of a benefit to the Empire to his own inconvenience, no matter how slight.

However, I submit that both men are making fundamentally the same point: namely, that a purely rationalistic, or *intellectualistic,* strategy in ethics is hopeless.

Of course, to reject a view of morality that is based wholly on the reasoning faculty is not the same as to reject rationality as a *factor* in morality. Clearly, rationalistic ideals such as the Golden Rule, doing one's duty, keeping one's promises, receiving one's just deserts, and furthering the common good, to name a few, all exert an unmistakable moral attraction. It is just that the systematic rational reconstruction of these ideals in formal ethical theories—such as contractualism, deontology, consequentialism, and so forth—cannot fully explain the existence of that moral appeal because *it is not purely intellectual.* This shows us that to strike the correct balance, we must combine the affective and the intellectual sides of the rational animal.

More precisely, it shows how our general viewpoint on rational agency and the human spirit—what I am calling "emergent rationalism"—can be further articulated in the direction of human *practical reasoning* by means of a strategy that combines the affective and the intellectual dimensions of the human form of being (or essence, or nature), which, as we have seen, includes the ontological foundation for so-called "second nature."

There are two principal ways in which this articulation must be pursued: first, at the level of "metaethics"; and second, at the level of "normative ethics." I will begin with metaethics.

8.2. Metaethics

To take the metaethical issues first, I will make a further distinction between: (1) *explaining* the place of normativity, or normative force,

within nature, in a general way; and (2) *justifying* the special normative force of *moral imperatives,* as such.

The general problem of normativity has already been dealt with
at some length in chapter 5 above. The human practical reasoner is
a rational agent who inherits the sentient and the vital aspects of his
nature from the sentient agency, and from the natural agency as such,
that he necessarily carries within himself. For, the human practical
reasoner is essentially a sentient agent to which has been added the
gifts of language, intellect, and spirit. Therefore, all these features
of human nature are "always already" inherently agential, which is
to say, teleological, evaluative, and normative (in the instrumental
sense).

This is an important point to remember in any discussion of the
foundations of ethics. It is too often lost sight of by those advancing
putatively "naturalistic" approaches to ethics, such as the elimina-
tionist and reductionist strategies alluded to above, or so-called
"non-cognitivist" strategies such as "emotivism" (or "expressivism")
which reduces moral theory from the level of propositional discourse
to that of purely emotional response. According to this doctrine,
"right" is whatever makes me say "Hooray!" and "wrong" is whatever makes me say "Boo!"

The Hungarian moral and political philosopher, Aurel Kolnai,
pointed out the fallacy involved in this sort of reasoning some time
ago:[6]

> [E]ven though value criteria like the pleasure, desire, preference,
> will or decision of the subject (or of a community of subjects
> to which he belongs) undoubtedly are naturalistic in that they
> express prevalent tendencies of nature or appetitive facts recog-
> nized as sovereign principles (Emotivism itself is an anaemic
> species of Naturalism), they still do not in any way refer to Nature
> in a comprehensive and overall sense. Nor do they refer to any
> concrete power or strength prevailing on the plane of brute factu-
> ality. Rather, hedonistic criteria connote an aspect of autonomous
> *evaluation* and thereby the hint of a departure from pure Natural-
> ism. (original emphasis)

---

[6] Kolnai (1980: 15).

In other words, what ordinarily passes for "naturalism" in ethics is no such thing. Rather, so-called "naturalistic" metaethical theories —whether cognitivist or expressivist—beg the question against the reformed naturalist (as well as the theist or Platonist) by ignoring the fact that agential, and thus normative, concepts are already built into such supposedly "naturalistic" metaethical theories at their foundation. So-called "evolutionary ethics" might appear superior in this respect. But, in fact, the Darwinian framework is even more thoroughly question-begging in the domain of ethics than it is in biology. It simply *assumes* the existence of agential powers throughout. As demonstrated in chapter 5, Darwinism cannot *explain* even biologically generic, teleological or normative phenomena. Much less, then, can it help us to understand morality. Only a metaethics pursued within the framework of emergent rationalism would possess the wherewithal to confront this problem head-on.

With respect to the motivational force of the special kind of normativity attached to moral feelings, judgments, and commands, a chief worry will be that I have conflated the *attractive* force of moral motivation with the specifically *moral* normative force unique to the ethical domain, properly speaking. This is a fundamental issue and it is important that any reconstruction of moral theory along the lines of emergent rationalism be able to give a plausible response to it.

The correct way to respond, I think, proceeds along two distinct, but ultimately convergent, lines of reasoning. First, we have already seen that the notion of general biological agency advanced in this book employs a conception of the good which *already* contains normative force. Normative force, or motivation, is not something extra added on to agency. Rather, it is an inherent feature of the phenomenon. In other words, the normative force of moral imperatives or prescriptions is ultimately founded upon the fact that the normativity present in general biological agency is a kind of *force*. To speak somewhat figuratively, Aquinas's statement that "the good is that which ought to be pursued" is equivalent to saying that *qua* living thing, a human being is under the ultimate, panbiological constraint —which is *analogous* to a moral duty—of preserving himself in existence (both as token and as type) and so also under the *instrumental* constraint of doing what his nature tells him is *good* (*that which ought to be pursued*) in order to achieve that end.[7]

Now, while this line of reasoning shows that it is a mistake to assume, in general, an unbridgeable barrier between the attractive and the normative, it still does not explain the special *moral* form of normativity. This brings us to the second line of reasoning mentioned above. Namely, we still need to show what it is about reason and spirit that provide the *special* normative force of uniquely human *moral* feelings, judgments, commands, and so forth.

The short way of doing this is simply to observe that, for human beings, the attractive (the good) is bound up with free will, conscience, and the domain of spirit. We are *not determined* by our human nature to pursue only our animal impulses under the guise of the good (though, of course, we *may* do so). That is to say, we are not motivated to practical action by our animal impulses alone. Rather, for us, values and ideals emanating from the realm of spirit contribute to and shape what we are capable of seeing *as* good. A sentient agent whose nature is thus modified by reason and free will is capable of checking its inclinations, of deliberating, and of choosing what seems best to it, all things considered.

There is another point in this vicinity, as well. The whole reason why the pursuit of the good for the rational animal so often takes the form of an imperative is precisely because such pursuit takes the form of what we might call "multi-dimensional motivation," meaning, in effect, that it is open to true *choice* and is *not compelled* to act in one way or the other. The human case may be sharply contrasted with that of simple creatures with what we might call "unidimensional motivation," like, for instance, bacteria. Even so, the internal, agential connection between the good and the normative remains the same,

---

[7] This point in no way conflicts with the fact that for human beings our moral duty may lie in self-sacrifice. Nor is there any need of "sociobiology" or "evolutionary psychology" to understand the specific contours of such self-sacrifice. Rather, its ground of possibility lies in the internalization into each individual's psychic makeup of ideals deriving from the domain of spirit. Yet, the domain of spirit is wholly dependent upon the physical existence of humanity. Hence, life always retains its status as the ultimate value for living beings, including even ourselves.

from its simplest and humblest to its most-complex and -exalted manifestations.

It is this internal connection between all action of whatever sort, as such, and normativity that ultimately explains human duty, as well. Our duty to act so as to attain whatever ends we perceive as right carries a distinctively *moral* normative force for us because it derives from our desire to *be* a certain kind of p*erson, living* in a certain sort of *way*, namely, a kind of person and a sort of way that we consider to be virtuous, honorable, noble, and the like.

Thus, there are good reasons why morality is universally acknowledged to be a human phenomenon, even though there are clear examples among the other animals of what we might consider to be morally correct actions, were they performed by human beings. But however admirable we may find the reciprocal grooming, sharing of resources, care for the young, self-sacrifice on behalf of the group, and so forth, which are practiced by many of our forebears among the great apes, who are our closest living kin. Still, we do not hold apes morally responsible for their actions. For example, it is commonplace for male chimpanzees to kill the offspring of their mates by earlier *liaisons*. However, it would be absurd to put such a monkey on trial for murder. Why, exactly, is that?

Obviously, the reason is that our moral condemnation of the ape's action presupposes its ability to subordinate its spontaneous inclinations to higher-order ideals and to deliberate about the best course of action, all things considered. In short, it is *unfair* to condemn the chimpanzee morally because doing so is *ipso facto* to ascribe to the animal free will, which it manifestly lacks. Morality can exist only where there is cognitive access to the domain of spirit, and with it the capacity for conscience and deliberation—in a word, where there is *free will*.

8.3. Normative Ethics

What about the so-called "normative ethical" issues, meaning the systematic explanation of the specific nature and form of moral imperatives?

It seems clear that the view of human nature advanced in this book comports best with the classical tradition in the realm of ethics, as elsewhere. Moreover, it is encouraging for reformed naturalism that moral theory is the one field in which traditional philosophy has had a palpable impact on contemporary academic debate. I am thinking especially of the work of Philippa Foot[8] and her colleagues and students.[9] I suspect that many readers will be familiar with or curious about the work of Michael Thompson—unofficially, *primus inter pares* among Foot's followers—so it may be just as well to begin my discussion of normative ethics with him.

Thompson's main contribution has been the observation that, despite the official repudiation of essentialism by the Darwinian mainstream, biology nevertheless employs an irreducibly essentialist way of speaking and of conceptualizing its subject matter. This can be seen especially clearly from natural history programs on television. The narrators of these programs frequently say such things as "*the octopus* possesses a camera eye" or "in *the meerkat* mating may occur throughout the year." Thompson refers to such locutions as "natural-historical judgments."

Thompson's basic idea is to use natural-historical judgments to ground the Aristotelian conception of the good, or *eudaimonia,* for a given species. However, as Richard Kraut has pointed out, this proposal is a non-starter.[10] The reason is simple: Thompson is approaching the problem from the side of human language and judgment, not from the side of nature. For the true Aristotelian, who cannot but be a realist, it is the essential nature of each species which grounds our natural-historical judgments, not the other way around. Once again, we find a philosopher attempting to use the semantic tail to wag the metaphysical dog. Kraut urges (though he does nothing to supply) what he styles a "bottom-up" version of Aristotelian essentialism for ethics, in contrast to Thompson's "top-down" approach. To my

---

[8] See, especially, Foot (2001).

[9] See, e.g., Boyle & Lavin (2010), Buhler (2016), Frey (2019), Hacker-Wright (2012), Kraut (2007), Lott (2012, 2018), MacIntyre (1999), Russell (2007), and M. Thompson (2008).

[10] Kraut (2013).

knowledge, the only contemporary moral thinker who has attempted to answer Kraut's call is Parisa Moosavi.[11] The work of Christopher J. Austin (though not centered on ethics) is also relevant here.[12] Both Moosavi and Austin attempt to interpret Aristotelian essentialism in terms of evolutionary-developmental systems theory (evo-devo) and the new dispositional or causal-powers approach to the metaphysics of causation. As I have explained above, I believe evo-devo alone is insufficient to do the metaphysical work that Moosavi and Austin require of it. Still, their approach is a step in the right direction.

Like metaethics, normative ethics is a vast subject, whose detailed articulation and development in terms of the present project I must leave to others. However, I would like to say a few words about the best way to characterize a normative ethics founded upon the present philosophy of nature. First and foremost, such an ethics will be based on a non-Darwinian—which is to say non-reductionist—understanding of human nature. Secondly, as a form of eudaimonism, it must be distinguished both from the overly intellectualized, formal systems of normative ethics—be it contractualism, deontology, or consequentialism—and also from the various "non-cognitivist" theories, such as emotivism. As a view which attempts to hew between those two extreme modern views, the present viewpoint requires a label that will be suggestive of its intermediate position. I suggest "rational eudaimonism,"

Let us step back, then, and consider what else it would take to make rational eudaimonism work. One of the first things we must do is formulate an adequate response to those critics who hold that eudaimonism *in any form* is fundamentally self-regarding, whereas morality is, or ought to be, other-regarding. There are two crucial points to be made here.

The first point is that modern moral theory makes a signal mistake to the extent that it regards morality as primarily, much less wholly, other-regarding. I will refer to this viewpoint as "ethical modernism" for reasons that will be clear as we proceed. Ethical modernism stands opposed to most traditional ethical systems, including the

---

[11] See Moosavi (2018, 2019, 2020, 2022a, 2022b).
[12] See Austin (2019) and Austin & Marmodoro (2018).

ancient Greek and the ancient Chinese, because it rejects any form of eudaimonism or virtue ethics, which provide the bedrock orientation of classical ethics everywhere. Modern ethics rejects the traditional ethical orientation primarily because of its deep-seated disagreement with the traditional account of human nature—which is to say, because of its diametrically opposed philosophical anthropology. The ethical modernist, in effect, denies there is any human nature that is morally relevant and holds that the only virtues that count (on what basis?) are the other-regarding virtues of love, compassion, empathy, pity, caring, concern, kindness, and the like.

In contrast, the ancient Greeks focused on a constellation of virtues such as the famous classical quartet consisting of courage or fortitude (*andreia*), moderation or temperance (*sōphrosunē*), justice according to merit (*dikaiosunē*), and prudence (*phronēsis*).[13] As already mentioned above in passing, Mencius also posited four cardinal virtues, namely, benevolence (*ren*), righteousness (*yi*), propriety (*li*), and wisdom (*zhi*).[14] While the two lists certainly differ in detail, what is striking in the present context is that for both Aristotle and the ancient Chinese Ruists, the self-regarding virtues predominated over the other-regarding virtues. To be sure, both traditions acknowledge an other-regarding virtue (justice according to merit, for the Greeks, benevolence for the Chinese). Nevertheless, all the other virtues proposed by both traditions are self-regarding. Moreover, they all boil down to the basic idea of "self-restraint," "self-discipline," "self-control," or, as I shall be saying, "self-command" (*egkrateia*).[15] It is true that later on in the West, the classical or "pagan" virtues were leavened by Christianity with the three new virtues of faith (*pistis*),

---

[13] *Nicomachean Ethics*, II.7, 1107^{b}1; II.7, 1107^{b}5–6; V.1, 1129^{a}31–1129^{b}1; and VI.7, 1141^{b}9–10; Aristotle (2000: 32, 32, 82, 110), respectively. For philosophical reflection upon the traditional virtues, see Garvey (2022), Geach (1977), and Pieper (1966, 1997). For the historical context of modern disregard of the virtues, see Himmelfarb (1995) and McCloskey (2006).

[14] *Mencius*, IIA.6.5

[15] The *locus classicus* is Xenophon, *Memorabilia*, IV.5 (Xenophon, 1994: 135–138). Amy L. Bonnette translates *egkrateia* as "continence," but that is too recondite for my taste. "Self-command" not only expresses the meaning of *egkrateia* simply and forcefully, it also corresponds to the etymology of the Greek word.

hope (*elpis*), and charity, or love (*agapē*).[16] But even here, only one (love) is obviously other-regarding, while the other two (faith and hope) are arguably self-regarding. They, too, represent ideals of self-command of a sort.

The most pressing concern, then, facing any contemporary ethics (like rational eudaimonism) wishing to base itself on traditional and commonsense principles is this: On what rational basis might we urge the revival of the classical virtues of self-command? Note that we do not seek such a response to the critique posed by modern moral theory in order to *replace* the latter's emphasis on the other-regarding moral principles of empathy, compassion, and caring concern, but rather as a necessary *corrective* and *complement* to love and benevolence, as the ancient Greeks and Chinese well understood and as the man in the street everywhere well understands today.

I have found it helpful to conceptualize the relation between the other-regarding and the self-regarding virtues as occupying opposite ends of a spectrum of the virtues, that is, an *axis of virtue*, with self-command at one pole and compassion at the other. (See **Figure 1**.)

Axis of Virtue

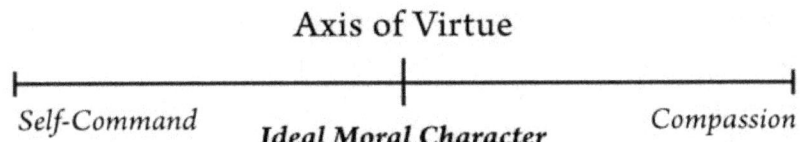

Self-Command   ***Ideal Moral Character***   Compassion

Figure 1: Axis of Virtue

Now, the two moral characters lying at either pole—that is, the one consisting of nothing but self-command and the one comprising nothing but compassion, respectively—are clearly defective. Undoubtedly, such pure character types are ideal fictions. Nevertheless, I believe it is instructive to take them into consideration. We may think of the former character, which lacks all compassion, as exhibiting the vice of *brutality* and the latter, which lacks all self-command, as evincing the vice of *sentimentality*.

Between the ideal types of pure self-command (brutality) and pure compassion (sentimentality), there of course lies an indefinite

---

[16] 1 Corinthians 13:13 (KJV).

number of mixed types. Which is the best mixed type will depend to some extent on such things as one's sex, one's occupation, and so forth. Generally speaking, there is little doubt that women's characters tend to skew to the right-hand, or compassion, end of the axis, while men's skew in the opposite direction. Both types are obviously needed by society, which is why they ought to be regarded as complementary to each other.

Abstracting away from sex, occupation, and other special factors, then, it seems intuitively clear that the ideal moral character is the one lying at the midpoint between the two extremes of self-command and compassion. If that is so, then, a fully integrated personality possessing both kinds of virtues will be more likely than any other kind to live a flourishing human life. It is worth mentioning in passing that this idea may be construed as an example of Aristotle's famous doctrine of "the mean" [*mesotēs*], according to which most virtues are located in an intermediate position between an extreme of deficiency and an extreme of excess (as courage lies in between cowardice and rashness).[17]

To return to the question of the fundamental reason which warrants reviving the virtues of self-command in this way, it is obviously impossible to treat this deep and contentious issue in the space allotted here with anything like the depth it deserves. For now, the following observation will have to suffice. The virtues of self-command are necessary as a complement to (not a replacement for) the virtues of compassion because the former are conceptually prior to the latter in a certain sense.

The virtues of self-command represent in a highly ramified form modes of habitual behavior that may be possessed in a much simpler form by all animals as constitutive capacities of their own various ways of flourishing. It is true, of course, that not all animal species possess analogs of all the human virtues of self-command. For example, the character trait resembling, say, fortitude, is far from universal throughout the animal kingdom. Many animals are timid by nature, striving to avert mortal danger through camouflage, fleeing,

---

[17] *Nicomachean Ethics*, II.2, 1104ª12–26; Aristotle (2000: 25).

playing dead, and the like, instead. But of those species that do ordinarily stand their ground or even attack when threatened, individual members who fail to do so will to that extent be less capable of flourishing as the sort of animals that they are.

To be clear, the moral here is *not* that the virtues of self-command have a longer evolutionary history than the compassionate virtues —neither form of virtue can of course exist in the absence of the human-style rationality, spirit, conscience, and free will. The point, rather, is that the virtues of self-command deal with the exigencies of living at a more elemental level—exigencies which, though extensively transformed in the lives of modern human beings, still impinge upon our existence today in manifold ways. It is for this reason that the virtues of self-command remain necessary to our well-being. In short, the exercise of the compassionate virtues presupposes the possession of at least some of the virtues of self-command, such as fortitude and prudence. If one is wholly lacking in the virtues of self-command himself, then he is in no position to give aid and comfort to other people. In sum, while compassion, empathy, and love may be necessary for the flourishing of the rational animal, they are by no means sufficient to wrest authentic and lasting well-being from the recalcitrant soil of this difficult life, either for ourselves or for others.

There are still other issues that would require investigation in a more extended discussion of rational eudaimonism. I have space here to mention only one or two of them. For example, it has been frequently claimed that no form of eudaimonism can explain the importance of the compassionate virtues and of concern for others, more generally. The reason is that the concept of *eudaimonia* was supposedly individualistic by its very nature. But, as Julia Annas has shown, this claim rests upon a mistake of interpretation:[18]

> In ancient eudaimonism my practical thinking is not about *my* interests as opposed to those of others; it is about how best to live my life as a mother, son, soldier, relative, employee, employer, and so on. Concern for others is already built in to my concern for my *eudaimonia*. (original emphasis)

---

[18] Annas (2017: 267).

I note in passing that similar conceptions of human happiness as perfecting virtue (or goodness), understood in a social sense, are commonplace in non-Western philosophical traditions, as well. For example, the great Mahāyāna Buddhist scholar and thinker, Nāgārjuna (d. c. 250 AD), defines happiness as follows:[19]

> Perfection in the path of goodness defines "happiness."

Here, too, it is obvious that happiness for the individual means the perfection of virtue with respect to others, indeed, with respect to all sentient beings. That is, after all, the very foundation of the Mahāyāna tradition.

In conclusion, ancient eudaimonism did not conceive of the individual person in abstract terms, as isolated from the *polis*, but rather in "thick" anthropological terms as already embedded in a system of social roles. There is no reason why a modern rational eudaimonism may not do the same.

Another issue we must deal with is the precise nature of the role of spirit in any contemporary reconstruction of eudaimonism as a "rational eudaimonism." In other words, we must spell out the precise contribution of the rational contribution to morality emanating from the realm of spirit.

There are at least two factors here: objectivity of viewpoint and objectivity of values. Very briefly, the first form of objectivity— of point of view—which is afforded us by spirit (as discussed in the previous chapter) has already been copiously discussed by the mainstream modern ethical tradition. It encompasses, at a minimum, Adam Smith's notion of the "impartial spectator"[20] and Immanuel Kant's various formulations of the categorical imperative.[21] It is, of course, also already embodied in the Golden Rule. As such, we may assume that it is a part of universal common sense, long preceding formal philosophical reflection upon morality.

As for the influence of higher-order constraints, I believe these are best conceived of as values and ideals, which possess a kind of

---

[19] *Rāja Parikatha Ratnāvalī*, 1.1.C.1 (Nāgārjuna, 2008: 31).
[20] Smith (1759).
[21] Kant (1996b).

objective existence in the domain of spirit, as discussed in the previous chapter. Value-theoretic ethics has been investigated primarily by the German realist-phenomenological tradition of the early twentieth century, which needs to be revived and incorporated into our present project.[22]

Thanks to the two-level structure of human agency, or "practical rationality," the classical virtues influence our moral conduct both from below—in the form of our instinctive motivations—and from above—in the form of the constraints imposed by objective values emanating from the realm of spirit. In this way, I believe rational eudaimonism is capable of providing a satisfying account of morality, while fitting in well with the general project of emergent rationalism outlined in the previous three chapters.

---

[22] See, *e.g.*, Hartmann (2002), Hildebrand (2020), Reinach (2012), and Scheler (1973). For a peerless, brief introduction to value-centered ethics, see Findlay (1970).

9. Political Community and the Natural Law

9.1. Political Theory and Scientism

Why bother about political theory at all in a book like this one devoted to constructing a contemporary philosophy of nature? The reason is simple: It is in the domain of politics that scientism is perhaps most pervasive and certainly most dangerous for the human spirit.

Accordingly, in the present chapter I explore scientism in two of its most basic political manifestations: (1) at what I will call the "metapolitical" level, in the form of legal positivism, which denies the existence of an essential human nature or any form of natural law based upon it; and (2) at the "normative-political" level, in the form of the modern, liberal-democratic doctrine of "neutralism," which absurdly pretends that a particular regime's preferred morality —libertinism—is free from substantive moral commitments.

9.2. Metapolitics

By now, it will come as no surprise to the reader to hear me say that the domain of the political ought to be viewed as emergent out of the general capacities of the living rational agent, and out of human morality, in particular. The primary additional factor which leads to the emergent level of politics is law, backed up by the threat of coercion. Law, in turn, derives from the specifically human form of sociality.

While political arrangements are to a significant degree histori- cally and culturally contingent, it does not follow that there are no universal principles at all informing all such arrangements. Not just anything is possible for human beings in the domain of the political any more than in the domain of the moral.

All human societies are constituted by various unifying principles, such as shared geographical location, kinship, language, history, and customs. This last principle, customs, implies a shared set of norms, mores, or rules. There is no such thing as a society unstructured by a system of norms and sanctions for violating them. All societies, thus, are governed by "laws" in the widest sense—whether unwritten or written—which constrain the behavior of the community's members by means of the implicit or explicit threat of coercion. To be sure, this coercion may take different forms in different types of societies. In small, face-to-face communities, it usually takes the form of the threat of harm to an individual's reputation, of shame, and, in the extreme case, of ostracism. In larger, impersonal societies, however, it almost always assumes the form of laws backed by the threat of physical force with which we are all familiar.

Another aspect of the political dimension of human society comes into existence with the advent of the settled living and population increase made possible by agriculture, the division of labor, and social hierarchy. In such large communities, the necessary planning for collective action and administration of sanctions that once took place through face-to-face assemblies consisting of most or all (male) tribal members, become unwieldy. Decision-making authority now becomes vested in a much smaller council of influential individuals or elders, or even a single chief, at which point we enter the domain of the political properly speaking. Most if not all human communities beyond hunter-gatherer bands are *political communities* in this sense.

I take the foregoing sketch of the origins of the political community to be an anthropological fact, by which I mean not just a phenomenon which occurs universally, in all human communities across space and time—though it does that—but, rather, one which flows necessarily from the essential nature of our species. Moreover, I take the fact that most human beings have lived and are living in political communities to be the same fact that Aristotle expressed by defining the human being as "by nature a *polis*-dwelling animal" [*phusei politikon zōon*].[1] All that is then required to apply the principles of rational eudaimonism discussed in the last chapter to the specifically political domain is to introduce a modified conception of *eudaimonia*, which relates to political regimes as opposed to individuals. We may refer to this shared form of *eudaimonia* by the political term of art, the *common good*.

So far, so relatively uncontroversial (I hope). However, I will now introduce controversy by stating that the substantive content we ascribe to the notion of the common good, or group-flourishing, shared by all political communities will depend upon our understanding of human nature—especially of the *kind* of social animal we take ourselves to be.

As we have noted repeatedly, the piers of our human sociality are sunk deep in the foundation of our mammalian and hominid inheritance. But, at the end of the day, this fact has little to do with evolutionary biology. It is one of the most salient and universal aspects of human lived experience. Hobbes's notion that humanity once existed in a pre-social state of nature of a "war of all against all" was always an absurdity and an insult to common sense. As the British philosopher and MP eloquently pointed out in a recent speech:[2]

> We were not born free; we were born attached. Before we make our own way in the world, we belong to a family. We are related before we are alone.

However, this commonplace must immediately be qualified by acknowledging that, as social animals go, human beings are only *moderately social*. That is, we are neither snow leopards, mostly going it alone, nor termites, subordinating our individuality entirely to the good of the nest.[3] What, exactly, does this mean?

Our inborn moderate sociality means that, if we are to be happy, we must live among others of our kind and form stable collective

---

[1] *Politics*, I.1, 1253a3. Obviously, we must abstract away here from the *polis*, or "city-state," as a specific, ancient Greek form of political community.

[2] Kruger (2023).

[3] *Cf.* Plato, *Statesman*, 301E; Plato (1986: III.55), where the Eleatic Stranger observes that the *polis* is not a beehive.

associations with them. While these associations may take a variety of forms, the possible variety is not infinite.

First and foremost, it is self-evident that human beings are *born into* such societies characterized by particular political regimes. In no sense do they *choose* the political associations they will be raised in. For this reason, the contractualist tradition in Western political philosophy that posits a primitive state of nature lacking political association is absurd.

Moreover, the genuine state of nature essentially involves not only political community, but also *hierarchy,* and does so for at least two reasons. First, children are by nature asymmetrically dependent upon adults. The Scottish philosopher John Haldane has expressed this point very well:[4]

> Because as a matter of practical necessity food, drink, shelter and hygiene have to be provided by others, and because as a matter of natural necessity initial language learning has to be social, a child takes shape, well or badly, under the influence of other persons. . . . The fact of the dependency of children upon immediate providers is part of human natural history so deeply rooted as to be proximate to, if not part of, the human essence.

Second, while small hunter-gatherer bands with a simple material culture are mostly egalitarian, as we already noted, agriculture leads to larger, more densely settled societies with a much more complex material culture. The inherent economic efficiency of the division of labor then ensures the functional specialization of such societies. Finally, functional specialization leads to the need for large-scale cooperation and coordination—which implies privileged leadership roles and social stratification in the form of asymmetrical relationships of all sorts, such as teachers and students, masters and apprentices, military ranks, bureaucratic seniority, and similar structures.

The political implications of these features of human nature are not far to seek. The political philosopher Yoram Hazony has expressed them as follows:[5]

---

[4] Haldane (2006: 585).
[5] Hazony (2022: 102).

Political obligation, whether to one's family, tribe, or nation, does not arise from consent but from the bonds of mutual loyalty and gratitude that bind us to the other members of such loyalty groups, including especially the past generations that built up what we have and handed it down to us. . . . mutual loyalty—which is largely inherited, rather than chosen—is the primary force that establishes political order and holds its constituent parts in place.

Moreover, Hazony's observations are no arbitrary construct attributable to specific characteristics of Western society. For the Chinese moral universe is founded on a very similar perception of the centrality of our biological being. For example, the anonymous Warring States period text, *Xiaojing* (c. fourth to third century BC)—known in the West as the *Classic of Filial Piety*—captures Hazony's idea in the simple observation that:[6]

Filiality is the foundation of virtue and the root of civilization.

However, even if communal living and social hierarchy in some form are non-optional for human beings, that fact by itself does little to help us distinguish better from worse ways of living together. For that, we need to bring in more conceptual tools, notably, the notion of justice. As Augustine of Hippo observed early in the fifth century AD:[7]

Remove justice, and what are kingdoms but gangs of criminals on a large scale?

The philosopher Daniel N. Robinson recently recast Augustine's memorable metaphor into a more academic form:[8]

In the end, a political regime is either justified or is a tyranny.

The question, then, is: How should we evaluate the many different kinds of political regimes that have existed, or might exist, with respect to their justifiability?

To begin with, recall that while the origin of human morality lies in the experience of family and group loyalty, still, as we have

---

[6] *Xiaojing*, chapter 1 (Makra, 1961: 3).
[7] *City of God*, IV.4; Augustine (1984: 139).
[8] Robinson (2002: 195).

seen, moral agency presupposes metaphysical freedom. This means that our collective way of living must allow scope for the exercise of at least a modicum of individual autonomy, if its moral foundations are not to be eroded by the abdication of individual conscience and responsibility. But how, precisely, are we to understand this demand for freedom?

One way forward is to notice that the importance of political freedom for the common good is analogous to the centrality of free will for the moral life of the individual. This structural similarity between the political and the moral good suggests an analogy between the "axis of virtue" previously described in the chapter on morality and what we might call the "axis of freedom." This axis would describe the varying amounts of freedom permitted by various types of political regimes, from a near-absence of freedom at one end to a near-absence of constraint at the other. While the analogy is not perfect, nevertheless parity of reasoning with the axis of virtue would lead us to postulate the politically best regime as similarly situated at the middle point between the two extremes. In the case of the axis of freedom, we may refer to these extremes as the poles of "collectivism"—which, in its predominant contemporary guise, might be termed "technocratic statism"—and of "anarchic individualism." Inasmuch as the main difficulty with individualism is its tendency to reject moral restraint and equate liberty with licentiousness, we may also think of anarchic individualism as being functionally equivalent to *libertinism*. The sweet spot at the midpoint between them I will call "ordered liberty." (See **Figure 2**.)

Axis of Freedom

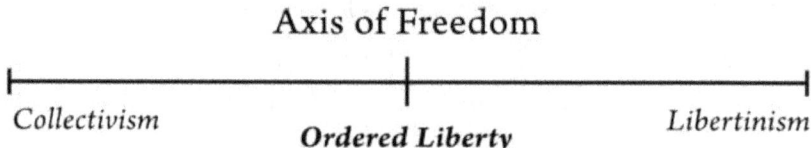

Figure 2: Axis of Freedom

The next obvious move is to represent the moral and the political axes together in order to illustrate how the ideal (in the sense of best) moral character and the ideal form of government (ordered liberty) influence each, producing together what we might term the "ideal society." We may do this by overlaying the axis of freedom upon the axis of virtue, then rotating it through 90°. (See **Figure 3**.)

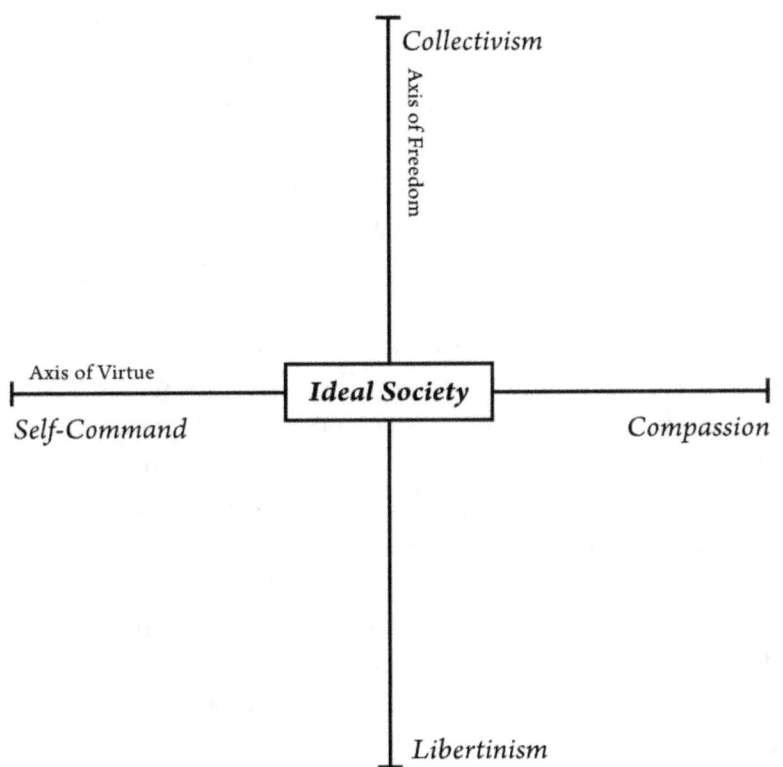

Figure 3: Ideal Society

There are, of course, many possible objections to this approach. Though I will have space here to consider only a few, here is one important objection to be getting on with: If we simply assume the metaphysical apparatus of rational eudaimonism, then we must assume the existence of the virtues and conscience, in addition to the positive law. But in that case, one might wonder: If the internal knowledge of right and wrong already exists, then why cannot political regimes be founded directly upon that knowledge? In short, on my account, why are laws necessary?

This is a powerful objection to rational eudaimonism. Luckily, the correct response is not far to seek. It is free will. The very faculty of the rational animal that opens up the entire field of right and wrong action in the first place permits human beings to behave either rightly or wrongly, just as they choose. Thus, the possibility of wrong action is built into the political domain through its very emergence out of the domain of morality. It is this possibility of wrong action by individual moral agents possessing free will that introduces the need for informal sanctions in fact-to-face societies and laws and physical coercion in large-scale ones.

Positive laws partially rectify internal deficits of conscience on the part of free, individual moral agents by supplying external normative constraints. But they can accomplish this only in part. For this reason, the stability and successful functioning of a modern, large-scale political regime featuring written laws and accompanying juridical and punitive institutions will still depend in large measure upon the *virtues* possessed by the members of that society. In other words, laws are required to *supplement* conscience where it is defective, but they cannot *substitute* for conscience and morality among a populace altogether.

Even so, there remains the further question: What is the ultimate source of law itself? This is another point at which the doctrine of ordered liberty has been subjected to withering attack. If we assume the positive law to be entirely conventional—as the great majority of legal theorists do—then why should those laws supporting a regime of ordered liberty be privileged? Why not, say, introduce a system of laws aimed instead at the material equality of all of society's members, for example?

To respond to this challenge, we must show that laws oriented toward ordered liberty are not entirely conventional, after all, but rather are necessarily based on an underlying natural law, which provides their ultimate justification. If that is so, then we will be able to see that those laws that are properly grounded in natural law in fact flow from essential features of human nature itself.[9] For these reasons, I submit that the best justification of a political regime

---

[9] For brilliant elaboration of this point, see Reinach (2012).

oriented towards ordered liberty lies in the revival of the classical theory of natural law.

I think we have already adequately discussed the evidence supporting the existence of an essential human nature. However, there are still two kinds of evidence for a universal human nature, relating to political regimes as such, which I wish to consider now. One is an argument from the universality of many basic human moral intuitions, while the other is an argument from morally justified dissent from positive law.[10]

First, to be clear, the concept of "natural law" is inherently universal in its application. One of the first great expositors of natural law, the Roman statesman-philosopher Cicero, lays heavy emphasis on this point:[11]

> True law is right reason in agreement with nature; it is of universal application, unchanging and everlasting; it summons to duty by its commands, and averts from wrongdoing by its prohibitions. . . .
> And there will not be different laws at Rome and at Athens, or different laws now or in the future, but one eternal and unchanging law will be valid for all nations and at all times, . . .

In short, the claim that there is a natural law is the same as the claim that positive laws ultimately rest upon the foundation of universal moral principles, where "universal" means instinctively recognized as valid by normal (non-sociopathic) human beings in all times and places.

In the eighteenth century, Montesquieu reaffirmed Cicero's point with this striking metaphor:[12]

> Before laws were made, there were possible relations of justice. To say that there is nothing just or unjust but what positive laws ordain or prohibit is to say that before a circle was drawn, all its radii were not equal.

---

[10] The distinction between natural and positive law was already explicitly recognized by Aristotle. See *Nicomachean Ethics*, V.7, 1134^{b}18–1135^{a}15; (Aristotle, 200: 93–94).

[11] *De re publica*, III.33 (Cicero, 1928: 211).

[12] *The Spirit of the Laws*, Part 1, Book 1: "On laws in general" (Montesquieu, 1989: 4).

To be sure, scientistic legal ideology ("legal positivism") rejects the existence of natural law and views all laws as merely conventional and context-bound. Nevertheless, legal positivists face formidable intellectual obstacles, because the evidence in support of the existence of natural law is overwhelming. This evidence is of two basic kinds: (1) facts about the universal scope of fundamental moral intuitions; and (2) facts about moral dissent from unjust positive laws. Let us look at each of these in turn.

To begin, then, let us attempt to identify a universal moral principle. I propose to examine the historical and cultural scope of one for which there is an abundance of empirical evidence. I am thinking of the reciprocity principle as expressed by the Golden Rule.

One of the first clear instances in ancient literature of a call for moral reciprocity occurs in the book of Leviticus, which probably reached its final form around 330 BC:[13]

> [T]hou shalt love thy neighbor as thyself

This command embodies the basic concept of reciprocity lying at the heart of the Golden Rule, but it does not yet explicitly invoke the notion of action or conduct towards one's neighbor. This element may be found in the apocryphal book known as Tobit (or Tobias), which was written some hundred years later, around 200 BC, give or take a few decades:[14]

> Do that to no man which thou hatest

This formulation was then filled out into the so-called "negative version" of the familiar Golden Rule by the Rabbi Hillel the Elder —who died, according to tradition, in 10 AD—as reported in the Babylonian Talmud:[15]

> That which is hateful to you, do not do to another

The more-familiar positive version is, of course, a central teaching of Hillel's younger contemporary, Jesus of Nazareth:[16]

---

[13] Leviticus 19:18 (KJV).
[14] Tobit 4:15 (KJV).
[15] Shabbat 31a (Bavli Shabbat, 2012: 145)
[16] Matthew 7:12 (KJV).

[A]ll things whatsoever ye would that men should do to you, do
you even so to them

Both Hillel's and Jesus's versions seem to be informing the anonymous, first-century Christian text known as the "Didache" [from the
Greek *didakhē*, meaning "teaching"]:[17]

[W]hatever you do not wish to happen to you, do not do to another

Around the same time, or a little earlier, the Roman dramatist and
Stoic philosopher known as Seneca the Younger (c. 4 BC–65 AD)
expressed a version of Jesus's positive version in his essay *On Favors*
[*De beneficiis*]:[18]

[W]e should give as we would wish to have things given to us

Regarding the positive and negative formulations, the early Church
Father Tertullian (c. 155–c. 220 AD) explicitly held them to be
equivalent:[19]

"And as ye would that men should do to you, do ye also to them
likewise." In this command is no doubt implied its counterpart:
"And as ye would *not* that men should do to you, so should ye also
not do to them likewise." (original emphasis)

The Golden Rule, in both forms, proved to be extremely popular. It
was an idea, as they say, with legs. It soon sprang up in the works
of a long series of Church Fathers, from Justin Martyr, Irenaeus, and
Origen in the second and third centuries, to Ephrem the Syrian, Basil
of Caesarea, and John Chrysostom in the Greek-speaking East, to
Lactantius, Jerome, Ambrose, Augustine, and Gregory the Great in
the Latin-speaking West.[20]

The Golden Rule also appeared in the Islamic world, beginning
in the twelfth century, if not sooner, when the Persian philosopher
and theologian, Fakhr al-Dīn al-Rāzī (c. 1150–1209), clearly articulated it in his *Tafsīr al-Kabīr*, or *Great Commentary* on the Qur'ān.

---

[17] Didache, 1.2 (Holmes, 2006: 163).
[18] *De beneficiis*, II.1(1) (Seneca, 1995: 212).
[19] *Adversus Marcionem libri quinque*, IV.16 (Tertullian, 1993: 372).
[20] Du Roy (2008: 89–92).

In the following passage, Rāzī is commenting on *surah* 83, which condemns defrauding by giving short measure in the marketplace:[21]

> Pay, Oh children of Adam, as you would love to be paid, and be just as you would love to have justice!

From these beginnings, the Golden Rule went on to become the common coin of religious and moral discourse for all three Abrahamic religions during the high Middle Ages and afterwards.

Now, the legal positivist might argue that this history does not really demonstrate universality. After all, all the instances cited so far of the penetration of the Golden Rule throughout Western Asia, the Mediterranean basin, and later all of Europe are undoubtedly historically linked, with the earlier instances directly influencing the later ones. That, of course, cannot be denied.

To this objection, I have two responses. First, at a minimum, we are entitled to speak of a remarkable *receptivity* to the idea of the Golden Rule within a wide variety of cultures. This, too, may be taken as an indication of the reality of the natural law.

Second, and even more tellingly, there is the fact that the principle of reciprocity occurs in cultures wholly unconnected to that of the western Mediterranean and Europe, thus minimizing the likelihood of direct influence by cultural "diffusion."

For example, the Buddha counsels basing one's actions upon mentally exchanging oneself with others:[22]

> Here, householders, a noble disciple reflects thus: "I am one who wishes to live, who does not wish to die; I desire happiness and am averse to suffering. Since I am one who wishes to live . . . and am averse to suffering, if someone were to take my life, that would not be pleasing and agreeable to me. Now if I were to take the life of another—of one who wishes to live, who does not wish to die, who desires happiness and is averse to suffering—that would not be pleasing and agreeable to the other either. What is displeasing and disagreeable to me is displeasing and disagreeable to the

---

[21] *al-Tafsīr*, 31:89 (cited in Homerin, 2008: 102).

[22] *Saṃyutta Nikāya* [Connected Discourses], Book V (*Mahāvagga*), chapter 55 (*Sotāpattisaṃyutta*), section 7 ("The People of the Bamboo Gate"); Bodhi (2000: 1797).

other too. How can I inflict upon another what is displeasing and disagreeable to me?"

In the Mahāyāna tradition, Śāntideva (fl. early eighth c. AD) wrote in his famous work, *Bodhicaryāvatāra* [Guide to the Bodhisattva Way of Life]:[23]

Whoever longs to rescue quickly both himself and others should practise the supreme mystery: exchange of self and other.

Moreover, the idea of reciprocity is very widely encountered in ancient Chinese ethical thought, beginning at roughly the same time it first appeared in the West. The Golden Rule shows up in each of the "Four Books," the oldest of which is the so-called "Analects" (*Lunyu* ["Selected Sayings"]), which was compiled over a considerable period of time, beginning in the early Warring States period (c. 350 BC), but which report the putative conversations of Confucius (Kongzi), who died in 479 BC. (Only much later, during the Song dynasty (960–1279), were the Four Books institutionalized as the foundation of education throughout the Empire.) In the Chinese case, then, cultural diffusion appears to be quite out of the question.

In the *Lunyu* we find the following clear articulation of the negative Golden Rule:[24]

Do not impose on others what you yourself do not desire.

Next, we have the *Mengzi*, or *Mencius*, which has already been introduced above. At first glance, the version of the reciprocity principle found in this text, which dates to 300 BC or a little later, appears rather different from that found in the *Analects*:[25]

Nothing will get one closer to benevolence than to force oneself to act out of sympathetic understanding.

However, the commentarial tradition informs us that "sympathetic understanding" is to be understood as equivalent to the negative Golden Rule as expressed in *Analects*, 15.4.[26] If that is correct, then

---

[23] VIII.120 (Śāntideva, 1995: 99).

[24] *Analects*, 15.24 (Confucius, 1979: 135).

[25] *Mencius*, 7A4 (Mencius, 2008: 172).

[26] *Ibid.*

the seeming difference between the two expressions of the reciprocity principle found in the *Analects* and *Mengzi* is more apparent than real.

Next, we come to the *Zhongyong*, known in the West for the most part as the *Doctrine of the Mean*. The *Zhongyong* is an anonymous text that originated as chapter 31 of the *Liji* [Record of Rites], which was probably written down around 200 BC. In the *Zhongyong*, we find our principle expressed with limpid clarity once more:[27]

> That which one finds undesirable when applied to oneself should assuredly never be brought to bear in dealings with one's fellow man.

Finally, we have the *Daxue*, known in the West primarily as the *Great Learning*. The *Daxue* is a very brief text that also originated as a part of the *Liji* (chapter 42). It contains this revealing extended discussion:[28]

> [B]ehaviour of the sort one abhors in one's superiors ought not be practised in commanding one's subordinates; and behaviour that one abhors in one's subordinates ought not be practiced in serving one's superiors. Behaviour that one finds abhorrent when observed in those with greater precedence ought not be practised as a basis for taking precedence over one's inferiors; and behaviour that one finds abhorrent when observed among those of inferior status ought not be practised in following the lead of those in more advanced positions. Behaviour that one finds abhorrent when observed in others, on one's right or on one's left, ought not be practiced in one's dealings with those on the other side.

This text makes clear that for the Chinese, the notion of reciprocity was naturally expressed against the background of the general Ruist understanding of morality as a system of proper conduct within the hierarchy of family and society at large. In the following passage, the distinguished sinologist David S. Nivison interprets the Chinese version of the Golden Rule as essentially a dual concept:[29]

---

[27] *Zhongyong*, 13 (Plaks, 2003: 31).
[28] *Daxue*, 10 (Plaks, 2003: 15–16).
[29] Nivison (1996b: 73).

(1) What I do *to* you, if I am in a *superior* position, should be
what I find it acceptable for you to do to me, if our positions were
reversed. . . .
(2) What I do *for* you, if I am in an *inferior* position, should be what
I would expect you to do for me, if our positions were reversed.
(original emphasis)

It is undeniable that this essential duality based on social hierarchy
produced a somewhat different interpretation of reciprocity among
the Chinese compared to the understanding of the Golden Rule in
the West. Even so, it seems to me that the Chinese conception
is similar enough to the Jewish-Christian-Islamic, as well as Stoic,
idea to provide clear evidence of the universality of the underlying
moral principle. And the universality of the principle of reciprocity,
as expressed by the Golden Rule in its various guises, is powerful
evidence of the existence of the natural law.

A different kind of proof of the existence of natural law is sup-
plied by the fact of substantive critiques of positive law—which have
not been rare in modern times. After all, in the name of what have
passionate critics of unjust positive laws practiced civil disobedience,
if not in the name of a higher law?

Frederick Douglass made this point with blistering eloquence in
an 1857 speech he gave two months after the U.S. Supreme Court
handed down its notorious Dred Scott decision:[30]

The Supreme Court of the United States is not the only power in
this world. It is very great, but the Supreme Court of the Almighty is
greater. Judge Taney can do many things, but he cannot perform
impossibilities. He cannot bale out the ocean, annihilate this firm
old earth, or pluck the silvery star of liberty from our Northern
sky. He may decide, and decide again; but he cannot reverse the
decision of the Most High. He cannot change the essential nature
of things—making evil good, and good, evil. . . .

Your fathers have said that man's right to liberty is self-
evident. There is no need of argument to make it clear. The voices
of nature, of conscience, of reason, and of revelation, proclaim
it as the right of all rights, the foundation of all trust, and of all

---

[30] Douglass (2016: 252).

responsibility. Man was born with it. It was his before he compre-
hended it. The *deed* conveying it to him is written in the centre
of his soul, and is recorded in Heaven. The sun in the sky is not
more palpable to the sight than man's right to liberty is to the
moral vision. To decide against this right in the person of Dred
Scott, or the humblest and most whip-scarred bondsman in the
land, is to decide against God. It is an open rebellion against God's
government. (original emphasis)

More than a century later, the Reverend Martin Luther King, Jr., too,
appealed explicitly to the natural law in his "Letter from Birmingham
City Jail."[31]

In short, the natural law is the conscience of society in its political
dimension. Thus, legal positivists are analogous to moral nihilists
who deny that conscience enjoys any objective validity in the life
of the individual. At both levels, the scientistic attitude leads to a
posture of pseudo-sophistication that denies the objective distinction
between right and wrong actions.

The legal theorist Heinrich A. Rommen once put this point eloquently, as follows:[32]

In real life this attitude [of amoral positivism] is untenable. When
he acts, and does not merely turn things over in is mind, even the
skeptic acts as if such a thing as natural law or objective justice
existed, as the common sense of ordinary men and women has
always implicitly held. And the reason is obvious. If anyone were
to attempt to realize a strict and consistent positivism in the
everyday life of society, his sole possible attitude would be an
unbearable cynicism.

To sum up, according to the meta-political theory on offer here, the
domain of the political is ontologically grounded in the domain of
the moral, while being emergent in relation to it due to the nature
of humanity *qua* moderately social animal. The best political regime
wiil be one of ordered liberty, understood as deriving from essential
human nature and expressed through the natural law. For, whether
acknowledged or not, the natural law is necessarily the ultimate

---

[31] King (1986: 293).
[32] Rommen (1998: 117).

foundation of all just political regimes everywhere. From it flow the fundamental customs and positive laws, both written and unwritten, of the best historically instantiated forms of social and political organization. The worst regimes are precisely those which contravene it.

9.3. Normative Politics

Let us now move from the metapolitical level of discourse to the normative-political, where a fundamental distinction may be drawn between two kinds of political regime. I am thinking of the contrast between "perfectionist" regimes—meaning those aimed at improving a society's overall moral tenor—and "non-perfectionist" regimes, which allegedly eschew such substantive moral aspirations.[33] The best-known exponent of the latter idea was, of course, John Rawls, who once opined that:[34]

> For the self is prior to the ends that are affirmed by it . . .

This explicit denial of an essential human nature is, of couse, absurd from the point of view of rational agency developed here. Still, it is a very widespread assumption of contemporary political theory. It is also perhaps the most-important means by which scientism has penetrated into the public life and consciousness of modern political communities. Therefore, despite its inherent implausibility, Rawls-style, blank-slate moral relativism, with its invitation to unconstrained social engineering, must be taken very seriously by anyone who opposes scientism.

For the sake of definiteness, I will discuss this issue of perfectionism versus neutralism in terms of the type of political regime known as "liberal democracy," which vaunts its "non-perfectionist,' or "neutralist," credentials. Liberal proponents of neutralism claim that all perfectionist forms of governance, which historically have most often been explicitly religious in nature, are susceptible to an extreme form of ideological zealotry, which easily slides into tyrannical collectivism. In contrast, they claim that the neutralist

---

[33] Hurka (1993), Norton (1991), Rasmussen & Den Uyl (2005), Rawls (1971), Sher (1997).

[34] Rawls (1971: 560).

form of governance is immune to this danger. The proponents of liberal neutralism further claim that only a political order based on their principles can justly govern a diverse citizenry whose members allegedly disagree about fundamental moral principles. The liberal claims that what he calls "comprehensive doctrines" have no place in the public square, inasmuch as their supporters supposedly rely upon a sectarian faith commitment, as opposed to publicly available reason, to advance their policy preferences.[35]

All of this is most convenient for the liberal. It places him upon the moral high ground of formal impartiality, while providing him with deniability, *qua* government official, for whatever substantive moral preferences he may secretly harbor. But if that is the way liberal neutrality was supposed to function in theory, it is not the way things have worked out in practice, as we shall see shortly.

How ought the perfectionist proponent of ordered liberty respond to this critique?

Regarding the charge that perfectionism may lead to tyrannical collectivism, it must be allowed that that is indeed a danger against which we must be constantly vigilant. However, no ideal political order exists, which might *guarantee* against this possibility. Certainly not liberal "neutralism," as we shall see presently.

Regarding the positive claims made by the neutralist, any effective response to them must encompass at least two sets of issues, one conceptual, the other empirical.

At the conceptual level, an old-fashioned classical liberal[36] might reply that to the extent that so-called "liberal" governments attempt to replace traditional values with their own "liberated" version of morality—in which the virtues of self-command are to be punished

---

[35] Rawls (1997).

[36] Note that even the father of modern liberalism, John Locke, still acknowledged the authority of the law of nature (*Second Treatise*, Book II, Chapter II [1960: 269]):

> [W]e must consider what State all Men are naturally in, and that is, a State of Perfect Freedom to order their Actions, and dispose of their Possessions, and Persons, as they think fit, *within the bounds of the Law of Nature* . . . (my emphasis).

and the corresponding vices rewarded—to that extent they are simply being untrue to their official neutralist commitment. If that were the case, then neutralism might still be defensible, at least as an ideal. However, in addition to the poor empirical record of self-proclaimed liberal governments in this respect, there are deeper theoretical problems with neutralism, as well.

For one thing, the doctrine implies a strong form of epistemological skepticism. But such skepticism is highly destructive of rational discourse understood as the pursuit of truth. In this way, a political regime based upon strict neutralist principles will be susceptible to the temptation of quelling political dissent through police-state repression. After all, if there is no such thing as objective truth, but only "our truth" and "their truth," then what harm can there be in coercively suppressing dissent, which *ex hypothesi* is lacking in truth?[37]

For another thing, the fact that the liberal ideal of public reason forbids commitment to any substantive conception of the good, or indeed of truth itself, means that liberal "neutrality" is just one more form of scientism, quite similar to the many other forms we have encountered throughout this book. It implicitly denies the premises of rational eudaimonism, human nature, and natural agency, all of which rely upon the insight that value is a constituent element of action by an objectively real, natural agent. Political agents are *agents*. As such, they cannot but act on the basis of reasons in accordance with values. No special additional proof of the wrong-headedness of the neutralist ideal is required here, seeing that this entire work has been oriented towards exposing its tacit assumptions as untenable. The very idea that an action of any kind, political or otherwise, might be "value-free" is absurd.

The standard response to this sort of objection is to distinguish between two forms of neutralism, one requiring neutrality in the *consequences* of government actions, the other requiring neutrality only in the *reasons* that government may cite to *justify* their actions.[38] The argument against neutralism from the internal connections among

---

[37] See the amazingly prescient essay by Willmoore Kendall (1960).

[38] See Kymlicka (1989: 884).

action, purpose, and value is alleged to tell only against a neutralism of consequences, leaving the liberal who adopts the weaker neutralism of reasons or justification untouched.

However, this feint is only superficially plausible. After all, the only reason any government can ever give in the final analysis to justify any action it takes is that it believes it will promote the common good. Therefore, it is analytical that value-guidance is a central feature of political action, as well as of action in its general form. These considerations leave the neutralist with no justification at all for his political actions.

It should be noted that the incoherence of neutralism is no minor or merely theoretical matter. It has had the direst of practical consequences, as well. Both indirectly, through the teaching function of the law, and indirectly, through the state-supported educational system, the decades-long, liberal flouting of natural law and pursuit of libertinism has systematically undermined the traditional virtues of self-command throughout Western societies.

As Yoram Hazony has pointed out, what we collectively honor and dishonor influences us profoundly. He makes this point in relation to religion, but it may be made just as well in connection with the virtues of self-command. To relegate the virtues to the private sphere is not "neutral." On the contrary, it sends the strong message that self-command is contemptible and belongs at the periphery—that it does not deserve a place of honor among the central concerns of our society.[39]

The result of Western societies' having pushed the traditional virtues to the periphery in this way can only be described as catastrophic. All moral discourse founded on the virtues of self-command is harshly condemned as "judgmental" and we are enjoined to employ the therapeutic jargon of the "helping professions" in its stead. As self-command has come to be despised in the West, in favor of an absolutist conception of "freedom," coupled with "compassion" as the only publicly accepted virtue, Western societies have grown steadily

---

[39] See Hazony (2022: 142–153; and especially, 144–145).

more pathological by all objective measures.[40] This medicalization of morality has worked hand-in-glove with the political project of "transgressiveness" (i.e., of turning traditional moral values on their head) to produce the social, political, and spiritual disaster we are living through today.[41]

This is an inherently unstable situation that cannot go on indefinitely, for as Edmund Burke acutely observed in 1791:[42]

> Society cannot exist unless a controlling power upon will and appetite be placed somewhere, and the less of it there is within, the more there must be without. It is ordained in the eternal constitution of things, that men of intemperate minds cannot be free. Their passions forge their fetters.

Only two years before, in his 1789 First Inaugural Address, George Washington, too, had predicted the consequences of rejecting the virtues of self-command and the natural law:[43]

> [T]here is no truth more thoroughly established, than that there exists in the œconomy and course of nature, an indissoluble union between virtue and happiness, between duty and advantage, between the genuine maxims of an honest and magnanimous policy, and the solid rewards of public prosperity and felicity . . . we ought to be no less persuaded that the propitious smiles of Heaven, can never be expected on a nation that disregards the eternal rules of order and right, which Heaven itself has ordained . . .

We cannot say we were not warned.

It is interesting to note, in passing, that a highly distinguished, contemporary Chinese scholar, Tu Weiming (b. 1940), concurs with Burke and Washington:[44]

---

[40] For *entrée* into the extensive literature on this subject, see, *e.g.*, McLanahan *et al.* (2013), Murray (1984, 2012), Popenoe (1996), Sax (2016), and Wilson (2002). For historical perspective, see Riley (2000).

[41] For the political context of these social developments, see Glendon & Blankenhorn (1995) and Sowell (1995). For philosophical defenses of moral judgments, see Robinson (2002) and Sher (2006). For a more empirically oriented defense of traditional morality, see Wilson (1993).

[42] Burke (1992: 69).

[43] Washington (1997: 732–733).

[44] Tu (1991: 449).

Social harmony and humane rulership are natural consequences of self-cultivation. Priorities are clearly established: only by strengthening the root (self-cultivation) will the branches (regulation of the family and governance of the state) flourish. If we reverse the order by first imposing peace on society with the anticipation that people will learn to live harmoniously among themselves, we not only violate the natural process of moral education but rely on an external political ideology rather than the trust of a fiduciary community. This is ineffective, for social harmony can only be attained through personal self-cultivation.

Finally, as of this writing (2024), supposedly "neutral" liberal democracy has taken a new turn, towards tyrannical collectivism. Over the past half-dozen years or so, we in the US (not to speak of other liberal democracies) have witnessed a level of unrelenting politicization of public administration, the education establishment, the mass media, and even the criminal justice system that effectively silences, and even criminalizes, political dissent. The liberal political hegemony still promotes anarchic individualism, or libertinism, at one extreme of the axis of freedom, but it now does so through tyrannical-collectivist means, thus uniting both extremes in a single political regime.

This seeming paradox is explained by the fact that the extremes of libertinism and collectivism both seek to destroy any residual moral influence emanating from religion, tradition, or the commonsense understanding of virtue and character. As the distinguished political philosopher Claes G. Ryn has summarized it:[45]

Social atomism and collectivism are somewhat different forms of the abandonment of the morality of character.

A passage from a late Warring States period Chinese historical text —the *Lüshi chunqiu* [Spring and Autumn Annals of Master Lü], dating from around 240 BC—beautifully summarizes our present predicament:[46]

Biased vision will cause the eye to go blind; biased hearing, the ear to become deaf; and biased thinking, the mind to become

---

[45] Ryn (1994: 135). Cf. the astounding prescience of Aldous Huxley (1932).
[46] *Lüshi chunqiu*, Part I: The Almanacs, Book 12, "Postface" (Lü, 2000: 273).

deranged. If all three of these are applied in a biased fashion, then knowledge cannot be impartial. If knowledge is not impartial, then good fortune will each day decline and the threat of calamity will each day increase. This principle can be seen in the fact that, once the sun's rays slant, it will inevitably set in the west.

In a nutshell, as a matter of historical fact, liberal neutralism has led to the victory throughout the West of the ideology of libertinism, which, in turn, has resulted in enormous increases in divorce, promiscuity, illegitimacy, violent crime, drug addiction, depression, suicide, and many other avoidable forms of human suffering—what once upon a time were called the "wages of sin." At least, they are the entirely predictable consequences of the dishonoring of the virtues of self-command.

For this reason, the pretensions of liberalism to be a value-free arbiter of a free society stand empirically refuted. The neutralist political regime has been proven a devastating failure at its fundamental task of promoting the common good. Its intellectual poverty stands revealed to all with eyes to see.

It is far closer to the mark to say that neutralism seeks to transpose legal positivism—which we have already identified as a form of scientism—from the metapolitical to the normative political domain. Therefore, the struggle against neutralism's essential moral nihilism is the struggle against scientism by other means.

Let us bring this chapter to a close by saying a few words of a more constructive nature about the sort of political regime that would—from the perspective of rational eudaimonism—best foster the common good in a modern industrial society. We have already said it would be characterized by that intermediate state of virtue and freedom we have been calling "ordered liberty." What else can we say about it?

Following the example set by the American Founding Fathers and other eighteenth-century classical-liberal thinkers, we may characterize the regime of ordered liberty as possessing at least these three qualities:

- *Conservatism*—recognition that inculcation of the virtues of self-command is essential for human flourishing; to the moral virtues we may add the political virtues of respect for the existing social order upon which we depend and of gratitude for the astonishing civilization we have inherited from past generations.

- *Meliorism*—recognition of the social order's flaws and of the need to remedy them, in part through legislative reform and in part by inculcating the virtues of self-command in all, thereby expanding the boundaries of the common good to encompass all.
- *Constitutionalism*—recognition that necessary changes in the positive law must be anchored in an unchanging constitution grounded in the natural law.

In summary, the domain of the political emerges from the domain of the moral by means of the natural law. The common good for such moderately social creatures as ourselves is to be found in the intermediate state of ordered liberty. This view is justified by facts about human nature, the natural law, and the internal connection between virtue and happiness. The best form of government for us will, therefore, be perfectionist—oriented towards the moral and spiritual, not just material, betterment of the populace—with safeguards against too great an emphasis on order at the expense of liberty.

More particularly, the best political regime will exhibit the qualities of conservatism,[47] meliorism, and constitutionalism, which form the core of America's political heritage—if only we can summon the courage to seize and defend it.

---

[47] Or "liberalism" in an older sense of that fraught term—the sense in which Friedrich A. Hayek said he was *not* a conservative (of the "crown and altar" variety), but a liberal of the "Old Whig" type; Hayek (2011: *passim*).

10. Conclusion: Spirit as the Heaven of This World

It is increasingly clear that for many of our contemporaries, "science"—always reified as a single entity—has become an object of veneration. Which is to say that for many of us, scientism now functions as a substitute for religion. This is the last aspect of the problem that remains to be addressed in our attempt to provide a comprehensive critique of scientism.

I do not wish anyone to suppose that I am advancing reformed naturalism as a *substitute religion* in place of scientism. The great historical religions of the world, east and west, are far better suited to human spiritual needs than any philosophical system of human devising could ever be. Rather, my goal in this brief chapter is to show that those who are attracted to scientism for quasi-religious reasons would do well to consider spirit as a superior alternative. That is, I believe that spirit can offer a form of existential solace—a "heaven of *this* world"—that is both truer to our experience of the world and also more comprehensive than that offered by scientism. After all, scientism's object of worship—the natural sciences—is only a subset of the domain of spirit. Here, too, as throughout this book, I am setting aside the question of the objective reality of a wholly transcendent ontological order.

Spirit, as we have been using the term, includes all the higher manifestations of human civilization. Thus, mathematics and the natural sciences, along with their applied offspring, stand alongside such achievements as literature, music, the visual and performing arts, history, philosophy, philology, and much more. While all these disciplines, both scientific and humane, share a common ontological status as inhabitants of the realm of spirit—and all of them are deeply imbued with the transcendental properties of truth, goodness, and beauty[1]—still, each one also has its own unique nature or set of essential characteristics. It is, above all, this inexhaustible wealth that makes spirit especially valuable as a source of solace for those capable of achieving some measure of identification with its boundless riches, which transcend by far the narrow limits of any single individual's experience.

To be sure, I have nothing like a logical proof to offer of the superiority of spirit over scientism as a source of existential consolation. What I do have are concrete examples of the attitude of some great thinkers towards the domain of spirit—examples which I believe demonstrate the enormous distance by which spirit outstrips the natural sciences as a source of solace.

For instance, the human delight in objective truth, goodness, and beauty is reflected in Aristotle's claim (I am paraphrasing) that the intellect (*ennoian*) is the most-divine (*theiotaton*) part of us and that, therefore, contemplation (*theōrētikē*)[2] provides perfect happiness [*teleia eudaimonia*][3] for human beings.

Aquinas seconds Aristotle's views on the intimate connection between the life of contemplation and human happiness in the enjoyment of the divine:[4]

> [U]ltimate felicity is to be sought in nothing other than an operation of the intellect, since no desire carries on to such sublime heights as the desire to understand the truth.

Plato, for his part, does not speak of "happiness" in this connection, but rather uses the stronger language of "love" [*erōs*]—notably, in the *Symposium*. More particularly, he says there that we transfer the love we feel for beautiful but mortal physical bodies to the immaterial

---

[1] That is, applicable to all categories of substance. The "transcendentals" are not to be confused with the "transcendent," which is the realm of being (if any) that stands wholly outside of the physical universe. On the transcendentals, see Aertsen (2012).

[2] *Nicomachean Ethics*, X.7, 1177[a]12–18; see, also, *ibid.*, X.7, 1178[a]5–8; Aristotle (2000: 194–195, 196).

[3] *Nicomachean Ethics*, X.7, 1177[b]24; Aristotle (2000: 196).

[4] *Summa Contra Gentiles*, III.50 (Aquinas, 1975: 174).

and imperishable "form" (*eidos*) of the beautiful (*kalos*).[5] Plato puts this doctrine into the mouth of Socrates, who in turns quotes his old teacher, the wisewoman Diotima. In this way, Socrates explains to the assembled drinking party in the *persona* of Diotima how it is that our lower nature leads us to a far higher way of life: the contemplation of the beautiful as such (or the fine or the noble—*kalos* can have all these meanings). Towards the end of the passage, Diotima employs this lovely metaphor:[6]

to polu pelagos tou kalou

For Plato, this "broad sea" is the world of the forms—what is often referred to as "Plato's heaven." I submit that Plato's heaven bears a striking resemblance to what we have been calling the "domain of spirit." The fact that reformed naturalism is capable of reconciling Aristotle with Plato in this way seems to me highly encouraging.

Many other thinkers and creative artists have testified to feeling a similar attraction and sense of consolation in contemplating the realm of spirit. For example, the 19-year-old Franz Schubert expressed it poignantly in this passage from his diary:[7]

O Mozart, immortal Mozart, how many, oh how endlessly many such comforting perceptions of a brighter and better life hast thou brought to our souls!

Another example of this frame of mind may be found in a famous work by the Chinese general-scholar, Lu Ji (260–303 AD). This text, known as the *Wen fu* [Rhymeprose on Literature],[8] depicts the realm of spirit as viewed through the lens of *belles lettres*. Here is the opening stanza:[9]

---

[5] *Symposium*, 206C–212A; Plato (2001: 37–42).

[6] [the broad sea of beauty—JAB], *Symposium*, 210D; Plato (2001: 41).

[7] June 13, 1816 (cited in Deutsch, 1946: 60).

[8] Literally, "*Fu* on Literature." The Chinese literary genre known as *fu* was a form of rhymed prose. The term has been translated into English in various ways, including "rhymeprose," "prose poem," and "rhapsody."

[9] Fang (1951: 531).

> Taking his position at the hub of things, [the writer] contemplates the mystery of the universe; he feeds his emotions and his mind on the great works of the past.
>
> Moving along with the four seasons, he sighs at the passing of time; gazing at the myriad objects, he thinks of the complexity of the world.
>
> He sorrows over the falling leaves in virile autumn; he takes joy in the delicate bud of fragrant spring.
>
> With awe at heart, he experiences chill; his spirit solemn, he turns his gaze to the clouds.
>
> He declaims the superb works of his predecessors; he croons the clean fragrance of past worthies.
>
> He roams in the Forest of Literature, and praises the symmetry of great art.
>
> Moved, he pushes his books away and takes the writing-brush, that he may express himself in letters.

As a final example, let us listen to the early-fourteenth-century Muslim jurist and theologian, Ibn Taymiyya, whose disciple, Ibn Qayyim al-Jawziyya, reported many of his master's sayings in his own books:[10]

> I heard the Shaykh of Islam, Ibn Taymiyya, say, "Truly, there is a Heaven in this world, [and] whoever does not enter it, will not enter the Heaven of the next world." And once he said to me, "What can my enemies do to me? I have in my breast both my Heaven and my garden. If I travel they are with me, and they never leave me. Imprisonment for me is a religious retreat."

In this way, two ancient Greek thinkers, a Chinese scholar living in the time of the Western Jin dynasty, a nineteenth-century Austrian composer, and a medieval Syrian theologian all employ kindred poetic tropes to express the supreme delight they feel in contemplating the objective, transcendental properties of truth, goodness, and beauty, which make up the ontological domain we have been calling the "human spirit."

To be sure, several (if not all) of these great creative intellects would see a wholly transcendent being as a far more important source

---

[10] Ibn Qayyim al-Jawziyya (2000: 57). I would like to thank Aron Zysow for drawing my attention to Ibn Taymiyya's "heaven of this world."

of solace than the heaven of this world. Still, I think they would all agree with me that, within *this* realm of existence, spirit and its contemplation by the individual intellect constitute the highest degree so far attained by the emergence of freedom.

Works Cited

Aertsen, Jan A. (2012) *Medieval Philosophy as Transcendental Thought: From Philip the Chancellor (ca. 1225) to Francisco Suárez*. Leiden: Brill.

Albrecht-Buehler, Guenter (2013) "Cell Intelligence" website, Northwestern University; http://www.basic.northwestern.edu/g-buehler/FRAME.HTM.

Alkire, Michael T. and Jason Miller (2005) "General Anesthesia and the Neural Correlates of Consciousness," in Steven Laureys, ed., *Progress in Brain Research, Volume 150: The Boundaries of Consciousness: Neurobiology and Neuropathology*. New York: Elsevier Science Publishing Co.; pp. 229–244.

Alkire, Michael T., Anthony G. Hudetz, and Giulio Tononi (2008) "Consciousness and Anesthesia," *Science*, **322**: 876–880.

Anderson, Philip W. (1972) "More is Different," *Science*, **177**: 393–396.

Anjum, Rani Lill and Stephen Mumford (2018) *What Tends to Be: The Philosophy of Dispositional Modality*. Abingdon-on-Thames, UK: Routledge.

Annas, Julia (2017) "Ancient Eudaimonism and Modern Morality," in Christopher Bobonich, ed., *The Cambridge Companion to Ancient Ethics*. Cambridge: Cambridge University Press; pp. 265–280.

Aquinas, Thomas (1975) *Summa Contra Gentiles, Book Three: Providence, Part 1*, translated by Vernon J. Bourke. Notre Dame, IN: University of Notre Dame Press. (The *Summa Contra Gentiles*

[Summary Against the Pagans] was composed between 1259 and 1265.)

Aquinas, Thomas (1948) *Summa Theologica,* translated by the Fathers of the English Dominican Province, five volumes. Notre Dame, IN: Christian Classics. (The *Summa Theologica* (or *Summa Theologiae*) [Summary of Theology] was left incomplete upon the author's death in 1274.)

Aristotle (1934) *Physics, Books V–VIII,* with an English translation by Philip H. Wicksteed and Francis M. Cornford. Cambridge, MA: Harvard University Press.

Aristotle (1936) "On Youth and Old Age. On Life and Death," in *idem, On the Soul. Parva Naturalia. On Breath,* with English translation by W.S. Hett. Cambridge, MA: Harvard University Press; pp. 410–427.

Aristotle (1970) *Physics, Books I and II,* translated with introduction, commentary . . . by William Charlton. Oxford: Clarendon Press.

Aristotle (1983) *Physics, Books III and IV,* translated with introduction and notes by Edward Hussey. Oxford: Clarendon Press.

Aristotle (1993) *De Anima, Books II and III (with passages from Book I),* translated with introduction and notes by D.W. Hamlyn. Oxford: Clarendon Press

Aristotle (1995) *Politics, Books I and II,* translated with a commentary by Trevor J. Saunders. Oxford: Clarendon Press.

Aristotle (2000) *Nicomachean Ethics,* edited and translated by Roger Crisp. Cambridge: Cambridge University Press.

Arnellos, Argyris and Alvaro Moreno (2016) "Integrating Constitution and Interaction in the Transition from Unicellular to Multicellular Organisms," in Karl J. Niklas and Stuart A. Newman, eds., *Multicellularity: Origins and Evolution.* Cambridge, MA: MIT Press; pp. 249–275.

Ashworth, Elisabeth (2014) "Terminist Logic," in Robert Pasnau, ed., *The Cambridge History of Medieval Philosophy,* in two volumes; revised edition. Cambridge: Cambridge University Press; Vol. I, pp. 146–158. (Originally published in 2009.)

Augustine (1984) *Concerning the City of God Against the Pagans,* translated by Henry Bettenson. London: Penguin Books. (*De civ-*

itate Dei contra paganos was composed in the early fifth century AD; this translation first published in 1972.)

Augustine (2012) *The Confessions,* second edition, translation, notes and introduction by Maria Boulding. Hyde Park, NY: New City Press. (*Confessiones* was composed between 397 and 400 AD; this translation first published in 1997.)

Austin, Christopher J. (2019) *Essence in the Age of Evolution: A New Theory of Natural Kinds.* New York: Routledge.

Austin, Christopher J. (2020a) "Contemporary Hylomorphisms: On the Matter of Form," *Ancient Philosophy Today: DIALOGOI,* **2**: 113–144.

Austin, Christopher J. (2020b) "Organisms, Activity, and Being: On the Substance of Process Ontology," *European Journal for Philosophy of Science,* **10**(2): article 13.

Austin, Christopher J. and Anna Marmodoro (2018) "Structural Powers and the Homeodynamic Unity of Organisms," in William M.R. Simpson, Robert C. Koons, and Nicholas J. Teh, eds., *Neo-Aristotelian Perspectives on Contemporary Science.* New York: Routledge; pp. 169–183.

Avital, Eytan and Eva Jablonka (2000) *Animal Traditions: Behavioural Inheritance in Evolution.* Cambridge: Cambridge University Press.

Baia, Alex (2012) "Presentism and the Grounding of Truth," *Philosophical Studies,* **159**: 341–356.

Baker, Lynne Rudder (2013) *Naturalism and the First-Person Perspective.* Oxford: Oxford University Press.

Barandiaran, Xabier E., Ezequiel de Paolo, and Marieke Rohde (2009) "Defining Agency: Individuality, Normativity, Asymmetry, and Spatio-temporality in Action," *Adaptive Behavior,* **17**: 367–386.

Barbieri, Marcello, ed. (2006) *Introduction to Biosemiotics: The New Biological Synthesis.* Dordrecht, Netherlands: Springer.

Barbieri, Marcello, ed. (2013) *Biosemiotics: Information, Codes and Signs in Living Systems.* Hauppauge, NY: Nova Science Publishers.

Barham, James A. (1996) "A Dynamical Model of the Meaning of Information," *BioSystems*, **38**: 235–241.

Barham, James A. (2011) *Teleological Realism in Biology.* PhD dissertation. South Bend, IN: Program in History and Philosophy of Science, University of Notre Dame; https://curate.nd.edu/articles /thesis/Teleological_Realism_in_Biology/24828495?file=43672 125.

Barham, James A. (2012) "Normativity, Agency, and Life," *Studies in History and Philosophy of Biological and Biomedical Sciences*, **43**: 92–103.

Barham, James A. (forthcoming) "Teleonomy, Teleology, and the Living State of Matter," in William A. Dembski and Michael Ruse, eds., *Darwin and Design: The Current Debate.*

Bar-Yam, Yaneer (2019) *Dynamics of Complex Systems.* Boca Raton, FL: CRC Press.

Başar, Erol (2004) *Memory and Brain Dynamics: Oscillations Integrating Attention, Perception, Learning, and Memory.* Boca Raton, FL: CRC Press.

Bauer, Erwin (1920) "Die Definition des Lebeswesens auf Grund seiner thermodynamischen Eigenschaften und die daraus folgenden biologischen Grundprinzipien" [The Definition of the Living Being on the Basis of Its Thermodynamic Properties and the Fundamental Biological Principles That Follow from It], *Naturwissenschaften*, **8**: 338–340.

Bavli Shabbat (2012) *Koren Talmud Bavli: The Noé Edition; Volume 2: Tractate Shabbat, Part One,* commentary by Adin Even-Israel Steinsaltz; translation under the direction of Tzvi Hersh Weinreb, Editor-in-Chief. Jerusalem: Steinsaltz Center/Koren Publishers Jerusalem.

Bernanos, Georges (1937) *Diary of a Country Priest.* New York: Macmillan. (Originally published as *Journal d'un curé de campagne.* Paris: Plon, 1936.)

Bhattacharyya, Krishnachandra (1983) "Reality of the Future," in *idem, Studies in Philosophy,* second revised edition, edited by Gopinath Bhattacharyya. Delhi: Motilal Banarsidass; pp. 635–

640. (Originally published in 1958 in the first edition of *Studies in Philosophy,* Vol. II.)

Bichat, Xavier (1994) *Recherches physiologiques sur la vie et la mort (première partie) et autres textes,* with introduction and notes by André Pichot. Paris: GF-Flammarion. (Originally published as *Recherches physiologiques sur la vie et la mort* [Physiological Researches on Life and Death]. Paris: Brosson, Gabon et Cie., 1800.)

Biro, Dora, Tatyana Humle, Kathelijne Koops, Claudia Sousa, Misato Hayashi, and Tetsuro Matsuzawa (2010) "Chimpanzee Mothers at Bossou, Guinea Carry the Mummified Remains of Their Dead Infants," *Current Biology,* **20**: R351–R352.

Blasone, Massimo, Petr Jizba, and Giuseppe Vitiello (2011) *Quantum Field Theory and Its Macroscopic Manifestations: Boson Condensation, Ordered Patterns and Topological Defects.* London: Imperial College Press.

Blitz, David (1992) *Emergent Evolution: Qualitative Novelty and the Levels of Reality.* Dordrecht, Netherlands: Springer Science+Business Media, B.V.

Bloom, Irene (1997) "Human Nature and Biological Nature in Mencius," *Philosophy East and West,* **47**: 21–32.

Bobzien, Susanne (1999) *Determinism and Freedom in Stoic Philosophy.* Oxford: Oxford University Press.

Bodhi, Bikku, trans. (2000) *The Connected Discourses of the Buddha: A Translation of the* Saṃyutta Nikāya. Boston: Wisdom Publications. (A part of the Sutta Piṭaka of the Pāli canon, the Saṃyutta Nikāya probably dates to around the first century BC.)

Bogdan, Radu J. (2013) *Mindvaults: Sociocultural Grounds for Pretending and Imagining.* Cambridge, MA; MIT Press.

Bonhomme, Vincent, Cécile Stquet, Javier Montupil, Aline Defresne, Murielle Kirsch, Charlotte Martial, Audrey Vanhaudenhuyse, Camille Chatelle, Stephen Karl Larroque, Federico Raimondo, Athena Demertzi, Olivier Bodart, Steven Laureys, and Olivia Grosseries (2019) "General Anesthesia: A Probe to Explore Consciousness," *Frontiers in Systems Neuroscience,* **13**: article 36; doi:10.3389/fnsys.2019.00036.

Bonner, John Tyler (2009) *The Social Amoebae: The Biology of Cellular Slime Molds.* Princeton, NJ: Princeton University Press.

Boswell, James (1980) *Life of Johnson, LL.D.* Oxford: Oxford University Press. (First edition: London: Henry Baldwin for Charles Dilly, 1791.)

Bouchard, Denis (2013) *The Nature and Origin of Language.* Oxford: Oxford University Press.

Bouchard, Denis (2021) "Three Concepts of Nativism and the Faculty of Language," *Language Sciences,* **85**: 101384.

Boutroux, Émile (1912) "Preface," in *idem, The Beyond That is Within,* translated by Jonathan Nield. Cambridge: Cambridge University Press.

Boutroux, Émile (1918) *The Relation between Thought and Action from the German and from the Classical Point of View.* Cambridge: Cambridge University Press. (Originally delivered in English as the Herbert Spencer Lecture at Oxford on October 20, 1917.)

Boutroux, Émile (1920) *The Contingency of the Laws of Nature,* translated by Fred Rothwell. Chicago and London: Open Court Publishing Company. (Originally published as *De la contingence des lois de la nature.* Paris: Germer Baillière, 1874.)

Boyle, Matthew and Douglas Lavin (2010) "Goodness and Desire," in Serio Tenenbaum, ed., *Desire, Practical Reason, and the Good.* Oxford: Oxford University Press; pp. 161–201.

Brading, Katherine and Elena Castellani, eds. (2003) *Symmetries in Physics: Philosophical Reflections.* Cambridge: Cambridge University Press.

Brann, Eva T. (1993) *The World of the Imagination: Sum and Substance.* Lanham, MD: Rowman & Littlefield.

Broad, C.D. (1923) *Scientific Thought.* London: Routledge and Kegan Paul.

Buhler, Keith (2016) *Becoming What We Are: Virtue and Practical Wisdom as Natural Ends,* PhD dissertation. Lexington, KY: Department of Philosophy, University of Kentucky; https://uknowledge.uky.edu/philosophy_etds/13/.

Bunge, Mario (1974–1989) *Treatise on Basic Philosophy*, eight volumes. Dordrecht, Netherlands: D. Reidel Publishing Co.

Burke, Edmund (1992) "A Letter to a Member of the National Assembly," in *idem, Further Reflections on the Revolution in France*. Indianapolis, IN: Liberty Fund; pp. 27–72. (Originally published in 1791.)

Burley, Walter (2000) *On the Purity of the Art of Logic: The Shorter and the Longer Treatises*, translated by Paul Vincent Spade. New Haven, CT: Yale University Press. (Composed in the 1320s.)

Burns, Robert (1993) *Selected Poems*, edited by Carol McGuirk. London: Penguin Books.

Burnyeat, Myles F. (2008) *Aristotle's Divine Intellect*. Milwaukee: Marquette University Press.

Butler, Joseph (2017) *Fifteen Sermons and Other Writings on Ethics*, edited by David McNaughton. Oxford: Oxford University Press. (*Fifteen Sermons Preached at the Rolls Chapel* was originally published in 1726.)

Buzsáki, György (2006) *Rhythms of the Brain*. Oxford: Oxford University Press.

Camazine, Scott, Jean-Louis Deneubourg, Nigel R. Franks, James Sneyd, Guy Theraulaz, and Eric Bonabeau (2001). *Self-Organization in Biological Systems*. Princeton, NJ: Princeton University Press.

Čapek, Milič (1961) *The Philosophical Impact of Contemporary Physics*. New York: D. Van Nostrand Company.

Cartwright, Nancy (1983) *How the Laws of Physics Lie*. Oxford: Oxford University Press.

Cartwright, Nancy (1989) *Nature's Capacities and Their Measurement*. Oxford: Oxford University Press.

Castellani, Elena, ed. (1998) *Interpreting Bodies: Classical and Quantum Objects in Modern Physics*. Princeton, NJ: Princeton University Press.

Chalmers, David J. (1996) *The Conscious Mind: In Search of a Fundamental Theory*. Oxford: Oxford University Press.

Chemero, Anthony (2009) *Radical Embodied Cognitive Science*. Cambridge, MA: Bradford Books/MIT Press.

Chong, Isis and Robert W. Proctor (2020) "On the Evolution of a Radical Concept: Affordances According to Gibson and Their Subsequent Use and Development," *Perspectives on Psychological Science*, **15**: 117–132.

Cicero, Marcus Tullius (1928) *On the Republic; On the Laws*, translated by Clinton Walker Keyes. Cambridge, MA: Harvard University Press. (*De re publica* was composed between 54 and 51 BC.)

Clark, Kelly James, ed. (2016) *The Blackwell Companion to Naturalism*. Hoboken, NJ: John Wiley & Sons, Inc.

Confucius (1979) *The Analects*, translated by D.C. Lau. London: Penguin Books.

Cornish-Bowden, Athel (2006) "Putting the Systems Back into Systems Biology," *Perspectives in Biology and Medicine*, **49**: 475–489.

Cross, Richard (2012) "Angelic Time and Motion: Bonaventure to Duns Scotus," in Tobias Hoffmann, ed., *A Companion to Angels in Medieval Philosophy*. Leiden, Netherlands: Brill Academic Publishers; pp. 117–147.

Cua, Antonio S. (2003) "*Yi (I)* and *Li*: Rightness and Rites," in *idem*, ed., *Encyclopedia of Chinese Philosophy*. New York: Routledge.

Curie, Pierre (1894) "Sur la symétrie dans les phénomènes physiques, symétrie d'un champ électrique et d'un champ magnétique," *Journal de Physique Théorique et Appliquée*, third series, **3**: 393–415.

Dasti, Matthew R. and Edwin F. Bryant, eds. (2013) *Free Will, Agency, and Selfhood in Indian Philosophy*. Oxford: Oxford University Press.

Davidson, Herbert A. (1992) *Alfarabi, Avicenna, and Averroes, on Intellect: Their Cosmologies, Theories of the Active Intellect, and Theories of Human Intellect*. New York: Oxford University Press.

De Caro, Mario (2015) "Realism, Common Sense, and Science," *Monist*, **98**: 197–214.

Denbigh, Kenneth G. (1975) *An Inventive Universe*. New York: George Braziller.

Denbigh, Kenneth G. (1981) *Three Concepts of Time.* Berlin: Springer-Verlag.

de Ridder, Joeren, Rik Peels, and René van Woudenberg, eds. (2018) *Scientism: Prospects and Problems.* Oxford: Oxford University Press.

Deutsch, Otto Erich (1946) *Schubert: A Documentary Biography,* translated by Eric Blom. London: J.M. Dent & Sons. (Originally published as *Franz Schubert: Die Dokumente seines Lebens.* Munich: Georg Müller Verlag, 1914.)

Dihle, Albrecht (1982) *The Theory of Will in Classical Antiquity.* Berkeley: University of California Press. (Originally published as *Die Vorstellung vom Willen in der Antike.* Göttingen: Vandenhoeck & Ruprecht, 1982.)

Di Paolo, Ezequiel A., Thomas Buhrmann, and Xabier Barandiaran (2017). *Sensorimotor Life: An Enactive Proposal.* Oxford: Oxford University Press.

Dostoyevsky, Fyodor (2008) *Demons,* translated by Robert A. Maguire. London: Penguin Classics. (Originally published in serial form as *Besy* in *Russkiy Vestnik* [Russian Messenger] in Moscow in 1871–1872.)

Douglass, Frederick (2016) "The Dred Scott Decision," in *idem, The Portable Frederick Douglass,* edited by John Stauffer and Henry Louis Gates, Jr. New York: Penguin Books; pp. 248–268. ("The Dred Scott Decision" was a speech delivered in New York City "on the Occasion of the Anniversary of the American Abolition Society" in May of 1857; it was first published later that same year by the printer C.P. Dewey in Rochester, New York, as part of a pamphlet entitled *Two Speeches by Frederick Douglass.*)

Du Roy, Olivier (2008) "The Golden Rule as the Law of Nature: From Origen to Martin Luther," in Jacob Neusner and Bruce Chilton, eds., *The Golden Rule: The Ethics of Reciprocity in World Religions.* London: Continuum; pp. 88–98.

Edwards, Richard (1962) *The Field of Stones: A Study of the Art of Shen Chou (1427–1509).* Washington, DC: Smithsonian Institution/Freer Gallery of Art.

Elek, Gábor and Miklós Müller (2013) "The Living Matter according to Ervin Bauer (1890–1938), (on the 75th Anniversary of his Tragic Death) (History)," *Acta Physiologica Hungarica,* **100**: 124–132.

Ellis, George (2016) *How Can Physics Underlie the Mind? Top-Down Causation in the Human Context.* Berlin: Springer-Verlag.

Emmeche, Claus and Kalevi Kull, eds. (2011) *Towards a Semiotic Biology: Life is the Action of Signs.* London: Imperial College Press.

Engel, Andreas K. and Pascal Fries (2015) "Neuronal Oscillations, Coherence, and Consciousness," in Steven Laureys, Olivia Gosseries, and Giulio Tononi, eds., *The Neurology of Consciousness: Cognitive Neuroscience and Neuropathology,* second edition. San Diego, CA: Academic Press/Elsevier; pp. 49–60.

Engel, Andreas K. and Wolf Singer (2001) "Temporal Binding and the Neural Correlates of Sensory Awareness," *Trends in Cognitive Sciences,* **5**: 16–25.

Falkenburg, Brigitte and Margaret Morrison, eds. (2015) *Why More is Different: Philosophical Issues in Condensed Matter Physics and Complex Systems.* Heidelberg: Springer-Verlag.

Fang, Achilles, trans. (1951) "Rhymeprose on Literature: The *Wên-fu* of Lu Chi (A.D. 261–303)," *Harvard Journal of Asiatic Studies,* **14**: 527–566. (Reprinted several times in anthologies of English translations of Chinese literature.) (The *Wen fu* was originally composed c. 302 AD.)

Favareau, Donald, ed. (2010) *Essential Readings in Biosemiotics: Anthology and Commentary.* New York: Springer-Verlag New York.

Feser, Edward (2019) *Aristotle's Revenge: The Metaphysical Foundations of Physical and Biological Science.* Neunkirchen-Seelscheid, Germany: editiones scholasticae.

Findlay, J.N. (1970). *Axiological Ethics.* London: Macmillan and Co., Ltd.

Foot, Philippa (2001) *Natural Goodness.* Oxford: Oxford University Press.

Fox, Rory (2006) *Time and Eternity in Mid-Thirteenth Century Thought.* Oxford: Oxford University Press.

Frankfurt, Harry G. (1969) "Alternative Possibilities and Moral Responsibility," *Journal of Philosophy,* **66**: 829–839.

Franklin, Christopher Evan (2015) "Everyone Thinks That an Ability to Do Otherwise is Necessary for Free Will and Moral Responsibility," *Philosophical Studies,* **172**: 2091–2107.

Freeman, Walter J. (2001) *How Brains Make Up Their Minds.* New York: Columbia University Press.

Freeman, Walter J. and Giuseppe Vitiello (2006) "Nonlinear Brain Dynamics as Macroscopic Manifestations of Underlying Many-Body Field Dynamics," *Physics of Life Reviews,* **3**: 93–119.

Frege, Gottlob (1997) "Thought," in idem, *The Frege Reader,* edited by Michael Beaney. Malden, MA: Blackwell Publishing, pp. 325–245. (Originally published as "Der Gedanke. Eine logische Untersuchung" in *Beiträge zur Philosophie des deutschen Idealismus,* 1918, **1**: 58–77.)

Frey, Jennifer A. (2019) "Neo-Aristotelian Ethical Naturalism," in Tom Angier, ed., *The Cambridge Companion to Natural Law Ethics.* Cambridge: Cambridge University Press; pp. 92–109.

Frost, Gloria (2010) "Thomas Aquinas on the Perpetual Truth of Essential Propositions," *History of Philosophy Quarterly,* **27**: 197–213.

Fulda, Fermin C. (2020) "Biopsychism: Life between Computation and Cognition," *Interdisciplinary Science Reviews,* **45**: 315–330.

Fuqua, Jonathan (2021) "An Ecumenical Mooreanism," *Philosophia,* **49**: 2019–2040.

Garvey, John H. (2022) *The Virtues.* Washington, DC: Catholic University of America Press.

Gaulin, Bruce D. (2012) "Introduction to Inelastic Neutron Scattering," PowerPoint. Oak Ridge, TN: Oak Ridge National Laboratory; https://neutrons2.ornl.gov/ conf/nxs2012/pdf/ Gaulin_Intro_to_Inelastic_Scattering.pdf.

Geach, Peter (1977) *The Virtues.* Cambridge: Cambridge University Press.

Gentry, Brittany A. (2021) "Measuring the Present: What is the Duration of 'Now'?," *Synthese*, **198**: 9357–9371.

Georgi, Howard (1989) "Effective Quantum Field Theories," in Paul Davies, ed., *The New Physics*. Cambridge: Cambridge University Press; pp. 446–457.

Gibb, Sophie, Robin Findlay Hendry, and Tom Lancaster, eds. (2019) *The Routledge Handbook of Emergence*. Abingdon, UK: Routledge.

Gibson, James J. (1977) "The Theory of Affordances," in Robert Shaw and John Bransford, eds., *Perceiving, Acting and Knowing: Toward an Ecological Psychology*. Hillsdale, NJ: Lawrence Erlbaum Associates; pp. 67–82.

Gibson, James J. (1979) *The Ecological Approach to Visual Perception:* Boston: Houghton Mifflin.

Ginsburg, Simona and Eva Jablonka (2019) *The Evolution of the Sensitive Soul: Learning and the Origins of Consciousness*. Cambridge, MA: MIT Press.

Glendon, Mary Ann and David Blankenhorn, eds., *Seedbeds of Virtue: Sources of Competence, Character, and Citizenship in American Society*. Lanham, MD: Madison Books.

Goodall, Jane (1971) *In the Shadow of Man*. New York: Collins.

Graham, Daniel W., ed. and trans. (2010) *The Texts of Early Greek Philosophy: The Complete Fragments and Selected Testimonies of the Major Presocratics, Part II*. Cambridge: Cambridge University Press.

Hacker-Wright, John (2012) "Ethical Naturalism and the Constitution of Agency," *Journal of Value Inquiry*, **46**: 13–23.

Hacking, Ian (1983) "Nineteenth Century Cracks in the Concept of Determinism," *Journal of the History of Ideas*, **44**: 455–475.

Hagen, Stephen J. (2017) *The Physical Microbe: An Introduction to Noise, Control, and Communication in the Prokaryotic Cell*. San Rafael, CA: Morgan & Claypool Publishers/IOP Concise Physics.

Haldane, John (2006) "Family Matters," *Philosophy*, **81**: 581–593.

Hanna, Robert and Michelle Maiese (2009) *Embodied Minds in Action*. New York: Oxford University Press.

Harold, Franklin M. (2022) *On Life: Cells, Genes, and the Evolution of Complexity.* Oxford: Oxford University Press.

Harré, Rom and Edward H. Madden (1975) *Causal Powers: A Theory of Natural Necessity.* Oxford: Basil Blackwell.

Hartmann, Nicolai (2002) *Ethics, Vol. 1: Moral Phenomena; Vol. 2: Moral Values; Vol. 3: Moral Freedom.* New Brunswick, NJ: Transaction Publishers. (Originally published as *Ethik.* Berlin: Walter de Gruyter, 1926.)

Hartmann, Nicolai (2012) *New Ways of Ontology,* translated by Reinhard C. Kuhn. New Brunswick, NJ: Transaction Publishers. (Originally published as "Neue Wege der Ontologie," in *idem, Systematische Philosophie.* Stuttgart: Kohlhammer, 1943; pp. 199–311; first English edition: Chicago: H. Regnery Co., 1953.)

Hartmann, Nicolai (2019) *Ontology: Laying the Foundations.* Berlin: Walter de Gruyter. (Originally published as *Zur Grundlegung der Ontologie.* Berlin: Walter de Gruyter, 1935.)

Hayek, Friedrich A. (2011) "Postscript: Why I Am Not a Conservative," in *idem, The Constitution of Liberty,* Definitive Edition, edited by Ronald Hamowy. Chicago: University of Chicago Press; pp. 517–533. (Originally published in 1960.)

Hazony, Yoram (2022) *Conservatism: A Reconsideration.* Washington, DC: Regnery Gateway.

Hegel, Georg Wilhelm Friedrich (1991) *Elements of the Philosophy of Right,* edited by Allen W. Wood, translated by H.B. Nisbet. Cambridge: Cambridge University Press. (Originally published as *Grundlinien der Philosophie des Rechts*: Berlin: Nicolai'schen Buchhandlung, 1821.)

Hegel, Georg Wilhelm Friedrich (2010) *The Science of Logic,* translated and edited by George di Giovanni. Cambridge: Cambridge University Press. (Originally published as *Wissenschaft der Logik* was originally published in three parts in 1812, 1813, and 1816. Nuremberg: Johann Leonhard Schrag)

Hildebrand, Dietrich von (2020) *Ethics.* Steubenville, OH: Hildebrand Press. (Originally published as *Christian Ethics.* New York: David McKay Company, 1953.)

Himmelfarb, Gertrude (1995) *The De-Moralization of Society: From Victorian Virtues to Modern Values*. New York: Alfred A. Knopf, Inc.

Ho, Mae-Wan (2008) *The Rainbow and the Worm: The Physics of Organisms*, third edition. Singapore: World Scientific. (First edition: 1993.)

Hoffmeyer, Jesper (2008) *Biosemiotics: An Examination into the Signs of Life and the Life of Signs*. Scranton, PA: University of Scranton Press.

Holmes, Michael W., trans. and ed. (2006) *The Didache*, in *idem, The Apostolic Fathers in English*, paperback edition. Grand Rapids, MI: Baker Academic; pp. 157–171. (This translation first published in 1989.)

Homerin, Th. Emil (2008) "The Golden Rule in Islam," in Jacob Neusner and Bruce Chilton, eds., *The Golden Rule: The Ethics of Reciprocity in World Religions*. London: Continuum; pp. 99–115.

Huang Zongxi (1987) "Author's Preface," in *idem, The Records of Ming Scholars: A Selected Translation*, edited and translated by Julia Ching. Honolulu: University of Hawaii Press; pp. 41–44. (Originally published c. 1676 as *Mingru xue'an*; the "Author's Preface" was added in 1693.)

Hueschen, Christina and Rob Phillips (2024) *The Restless Cell: Continuum Theories of Living Matter*. Princeton, NJ: Princeton University Press.

Hume, David (1978) *A Treatise of Human Nature*, edited by L.A. Selby-Bigge; second edition, revised by P.H. Nidditch. Oxford: Clarendon Press. (Original publication: London: John Noon, 1739–1740.)

Hurka, Thomas (1993) *Perfectionism*. New York: Oxford University Press.

Hutto, Daniel D., Erik Myin, Anco Peeters, and Farid Zahnoun (2018) "The Cognitive Basis of Computation: Putting Computation in Its Place," in Mark Sprevak and Matteo Colombo, eds., *The Routledge Handbook of the Computational Mind*. London: Routledge; pp. 272–282.

Huxley, Aldous (1932) *Brave New World*. London: Chatto & Windus. (Numerous reprint editions.)

Ibn Qayyim al-Jawziyya (2000) *The Invocation of God*, translated by Michael Abdurrahman Fitzgerald and Moulay Youssef Slitine. Cambridge, UK: Islamic Texts Society. (Translation of *Al-Wābil al-Ṣayyib min al-Kalim al-Ṭayyib*, written in the second quarter of the fourteenth century AD; the Arabic title literally means "Torrential Downpour from *The Goodly Words*," that is, a condensation of the book [by Ibn Taymiyya] entitled *al-Kalim al-Ṭayyib*, or "the Goodly Words.")

Ingthorsson, Rögnvaldur D. (2001) "Temporal Parity and the Problem of Change," *SATS—Nordic Journal of Philosophy*, 2: 60–79.

Ingthorsson, Rögnvaldur D. (2021) *A Powerful Particulars View of Causation*. New York: Routledge.

Ivanhoe, Philip J. (2000) *Confucian Moral Self Cultivation*, second edition. Indianapolis, IN: Hackett Publishing Company.

Jablonka, Eva and Marion J. Lamb (2014) *Evolution in Four Dimensions: Genetic, Epigenetic, Behavioral, and Symbolic Variation in the History of Life*, revised edition. Cambridge, MA: Bradford Books/MIT Press. (Originally published in 2005.)

James, William (1956) "The Dilemma of Determinism," in *idem*, *The Will to Believe and Other Essays in Popular Philosophy* (bound together with *Human Immortality*). New York: Dover Publications; pp. 145–183. (Original publication: London: Longmans, Green & Co., 1897.)

Johansen, Thomas Kjeller (2012) *The Powers of Aristotle's Soul*. Oxford: Oxford University Press.

John, E. Roy (2005) "From Synchronous Neuronal Discharges to Subjective Awareness?," in Steven Laureys, ed., *Progress in Brain Research, Volume 150: The Boundaries of Consciousness: Neurobiology and Neuropathology*. New York: Elsevier Science Publishing Co.; pp. 143–171.

John, E. Roy and Leslie S. Prichep (2005) "The Anesthetic Cascade: A Theory of How Anesthesia Suppresses Consciousness," *Anesthesiology*, 102: 447–471.

Jonas, Hans (1966) *The Phenomenon of Life: Toward a Philosophical Biology*. New York, Harper & Row, 1966.

Joyce, Richard (2002) *The Myth of Morality*. Cambridge: Cambridge University Press.

Juarrero, Alicia (1999) *Dynamics in Action: Intentional Behavior as a Complex System*. Cambridge, MA: Bradford Books/MIT Press.

Kann, Christoph (2016) "Supposition and Properties of Terms," in Catarina Dutilh Novaes and Stephen Read, eds., *The Cambridge Companion to Medieval Logic*. Cambridge: Cambridge University Press; pp. 220–244.

Kant, Immanuel (1996a) *Critique of Practical Reason*, in *idem*, *Practical Philosophy*, edited and translated by Mary J. Gregor. Cambridge: Cambridge University Press; pp. 133–271. (Originally published as *Critik der practischen Vernunft*. Riga: Johann Friedrich Hartknoch, 1788.)

Kant, Immanuel (1996b) *Groundwork of the Metaphysics of Morals*, in i*dem*, *Practical Philosophy*, edited and translated by Mary J. Gregor. Cambridge: Cambridge University Press; pp. 41–108. (Originally published as *Grundlegung zur Metaphysik der Sitten*. Riga: Johann Friedrich Hartknoch, 1785.)

Kauffman, Stuart A. (1993) *The Origins of Order: Self-Organization and Selection in Evolution*. Oxford: Oxford University Press.

Kauffman, Stuart A. (2019) *A World Beyond Physics: The Emergence and Evolution of Life*. Oxford: Oxford University Press.

Kelso, J. Scott (1995) *Dynamic Patterns: The Self-Organization of Brain and Behavior*. Cambridge, MA: MIT Press.

Kendall, Willmoore (1960) "The 'Open Society' and Its Fallacies," *American Political Science Review*, **54**: 972–979. (Reprinted in *idem, Willmoore Kendall Contra Mundum*, reprint edition, edited by Nellie D. Kendall. Lanham, MD: University Press of America, 1994; pp. 635–649; first edition published in 1971.)

Kierland, Brian and Bradley Monton (2007) "Presentism and the Objection from Being-Supervenience," *Australasian Journal of Philosophy*, **85**: 485–497.

King, Martin Luther, Jr. (1986) "Letter from Birmingham City Jail," in *idem*, *A Testament of Hope: The Essential Writings and*

Speeches of Martin Luther King, Jr., edited by James Melvin Washington. New York: HaperOne; pp. 289–302. (The Letter was composed on April 16, 1963, and originally published in Martin Luther King, Jr., *Why We Can't Wait.* New York: Harper & Row, 1964.)

Kiverstein, Julian and Erik Rietveld (2018) "Reconceiving Representation-Hungry Cognition: An Ecological-Enactive Proposal," *Adaptive Behavior,* **26**: 147–163.

Kiverstein, Julian and Erik Rietveld (2021) "Scaling-Up Skilled Intentionality to Linguistic Thought," *Synthese,* **198** (Supp. 1): S175–S194.

Klima, Gyula (1993) "The Changing Role of *entia rationis* in Mediaeval Semantics and Ontology: A Comparative Study with a Reconstruction," *Synthese,* **96**: 25–58.

Kolnai, Aurel (1980) "The Ghost of the Naturalistic Fallacy," *Philosophy,* 1980, **55**: 5–16 (Published posthumously; the year of composition is uncertain, but the manuscript is thought to date to the early 1960s. Reprinted in *idem, Politics, Values, and National Socialism,* edited by Graham McAleer. New Brunswick, NJ: Transaction Publishers, 2013; pp. 251–263.)

Kondepudi, Dilip and Ilya Prigogine (2014) *Modern Thermodynamics: From Heat Engines to Dissipative Structures,* second edition. New York: Wiley. (First edition: 1998.)

Koons, Robert C. (2022) *Is St. Thomas's Aristotelian Philosophy of Nature Obsolete?* South Bend, IN: St. Augustine's Press.

Kozma, Robert and Walter J. Freeman (2016) *Cognitive Phase Transitions in the Cerebral Cortex—Enhancing the Neuron Doctrine by Modeling Neural Fields.* Cham, Switzerland: Springer International Publishing.

Kraut, Richard (2007) *What is Good and Why: The Ethics of Well-Being.* Cambridge, MA: Harvard University Press.

Kraut, Richard (2013) "Human Diversity and the Nature of Well-Being: Reflections on Sumner's Methodology," *Res Philosophica,* **90**: 307–322.

Kruger, Danny (2023) "Tories Must Trust the People," featured speaker, Nat Con UK 2023 conference, London, May 17, 2023.

Kugler, Peter N. and Michael T. Turvey (1987) *Information, Natural Law, and the Self-Assembly of Rhythmic Movement.* Mahwah, NJ: Lawrence Erlbaum Associates. (Reprinted by Routledge in 2016.)

Kūkai (1972) *Major Works,* translated and introduced by Yoshito S. Hakeda. New York: Columbia University Press, 1972.

Kymlicka, Will (1989) "Liberal Individualism and Liberal Neutrality," *Ethics,* **99**: 883–905.

LaRock, Eric, Jeffrey Schwartz, Iliyan Ivanov, and David Carreon (2020) "A Strong Emergence Hypothesis of Conscious Integration and Neural Rewiring," *International Philosophical Quarterly,* **60**: 97–115.

Laughlin, Robert B. and David Pines (2000) "The Theory of Everything," *Proceedings of the National Academy of Sciences, USA,* **97**: 28–31.

Laughlin, Robert B., David Pines, Joerg Schmalian, Branko P. Stojković, and Peter Wolynes (2000) "The Middle Way," *Proceedings of the National Academy of Sciences, USA,* **97**: 32–37.

Leander, Folke (1974) *The Inner Check.* London: Edward Wright, Ltd.

Leclerc, Ivor (1986) *The Philosophy of Nature.* Washington, DC: Catholic University of America Press.

Leibniz, Gottfried Wilhelm (1985) *Theodicy: Essays on the Goodness of God, the Freedom of Man and the Origin of Evil,* translated by E.M. Huggard, with commentary by Austin Farrer. LaSalle, IL: Open Court Publishing Company. (Originally published as *Essai de Théodicée . . .* Amsterdam: Isaac Troyel, 1710.)

Leibniz, Gottfried Wilhelm (1989) "On the Radical Origination of Things," in *idem, Philosophical Papers and Letters,* second edition, edited by Leroy E. Loemker. Dordrecht, Netherlands: Kluwer Academic; pp. 486–491. (Composed in 1697 under the title *"De rerum originatione radicali"*; first published in 1840.)

Lennox, James G. (1992) "Teleology," in Evelyn Fox Keller and Elisabeth A. Lloyd, eds., *Keywords in Evolutionary Biology.* Cambridge, MA; Harvard University Press; pp. 324–333.

Lennox, James G. (2017) "An Aristotelian Philosophy of Biology: Form, Function and Development," *Acta Philosophica*, **26**: 33–51.

Lequier, Jules (1865) *"Introduction,"* in idem, *La Recherche d'une première vérité*, edited and published (anonymously) by Charles Renouvier. Saint-Cloud: Imprimerie de Mme Ve Belin; pp. 1–8. (This *"Introduction"* later became known as *"La feuille de charmille"*; for an English translation, see "Jules Lequier's 'The Hornbeam Leaf,'" introduced and translated by Harvey H. Brimmer, *Philosophy in Context*, 1974, **3**: 94–100.)

Lindley, David (2004) *Degrees of Kelvin: A Tale of Genius, Invention, and Tragedy.* Washington, DC: Joseph Henry Press.

Locke, John (1960) *Two Treatises of Government*, edited by Peter Laslett. Cambridge: Cambridge University Press. (Original publication: London: Awnsham Churchill, 1690.)

Long, Steven A. (2010) *Natura Pura: On the Recovery of Nature in the Doctrine of Grace.* New York: Fordham University Press.

Longo, Giuseppe and Maël Montévil (2014) *Perspectives on Organisms: Biological Time, Symmetries and Singularities.* Heidelberg: Springer.

Lott, Micah (2012) "Have Elephant Seals Refuted Aristotle? Nature, Function, and Moral Goodness," *Journal of Moral Philosophy*, **9**: 1–23.

Lott, Micah (2018) "Must Realists Be Skeptics? An Aristotelian Reply to a Darwinian Dilemma," *Philosophical Studies*, **175**: 71–96.

Lowe, E.J. (2006) *The Four-Category Ontology: A Metaphysical Foundation for Natural Science.* Oxford: Clarendon Press.

Lowe, E.J. (2008) *Personal Agency: The Metaphysics of Mind and Action.* Oxford: Oxford University Press.

Lowe, E.J. (2009) *More Kinds of Being.* Chichester, UK: Wiley-Blackwell.

Lü Buwei (2000) *The Annals of Lü Buwei*, translated by John Knoblock and Jeffrey Riegel. Stanford, CA: Stanford University Press.

Lucas, J.R. (1999) "A Century of Time," in Jeremy Butterfield, ed., *The Arguments of Time*. Oxford: Oxford University Press, pp. 1–20.

Lyon, Pamela (2006) "The Biogenic Approach to Cognition," *Cognitive Processing*, **7**:11–29.

Lyon, Pamela (2016) "The Cognitive Cell: Bacterial Behavior Reconsidered," *Frontiers in Microbiology*, **6**, Article 264.

MacIntyre, Alasdair C. (1999) *Dependent Rational Animals*. Peru, IL: Open Court Publishing Co.

Mackie, J.L. (1977) *Ethics: Inventing Right and Wrong*. Harmondsworth, UK: Penguin Books.

Macphail, Euan M. (1993) *The Neuroscience of Animal Intelligence: From the Seahare to the Seahorse*. New York: Columbia University Press.

Makra, Mary Lelia, trans. (1961) *The Hsiao Ching*, edited by Paul K.T. Sih. New York: St. John's University Press.

Marmodoro, Anna (2013) "Aristotle's Hylomorphism without Reconditioning," *Philosophical Inquiry*, **36**: 5–22.

Mashour, George A. (2004) "Consciousness Unbound: Toward a Paradigm of General Anesthesia," *Anesthesiology*, **100**: 423–433.

Mashour, George A. (2013) "Cognitive Unbinding: A Neuroscientific Paradigm of General Anesthesia and Related States of Unconsciousness," *Neuroscience and Biobehavioral Reviews*, **37**(10); doi:10.1016/j.neubiorev.2013.09.009.

Mashour, George A. (2015) "Consciousness and Anesthesia," in Steven Laureys, Olivia Gosseries, and Giulio Tononi, eds., *The Neurology of Consciousness: Cognitive Neuroscience and Neuropathology*, second edition. San Diego, CA: Academic Press/Elsevier; pp. 139–152.

Mayr, Ernst (1965) "Cause and Effect in Biology," in Daniel Lerner, ed., *Cause and Effect*. New York: Free Press; pp. 33–50.

McClintock, Barbara (1984) "The Significance of Responses of the Genome to Challenge," *Science*, **226**: 792–801.

McCloskey, Deirdre (2006) *The Bourgeois Virtues: Ethics for an Age of Commerce*. Chicago: University of Chicago Press.

McDowell, John (1994) *Mind and World.* Cambridge, MA: Harvard University Press.

McDowell, John (1998) "Two Sorts of Naturalism," in *idem, Mind, Value, and Reality.* Cambridge, MA: Harvard University Press; pp. 167–197. (Originally published in Rosalind Hursthouse, Gavin Lawrence, and Warren Quinn, eds., *Virtues and Reasons: Philippa Foot and Moral Theory.* Oxford: Clarendon Press, 1996; pp. 149–179.)

McLanahan, Sara, Laura Tach, and Daniel Schechter (2013) "The Causal Effects of Father Absence," *Annual Review of Sociology,* **39**: 399–427.

McLaughlin, Thomas (2022) "Energy and Form," *The Thomist,* **86**: 1–51.

Mele, Alfred R. (2006) *Free Will and Luck.* Oxford: Oxford University Press.

Mencius (2008) *Mengzi, with Selections from Traditional Commentaries,* translated by Bryan W. Van Norden. Indianapolis, IN: Hackett Publishing Company.

Merton, Robert K. (1942) "Science and Technology in a Democratic Order," *Journal of Legal and Political Sociology,* **1**: 115–126. (Reprinted numerous times under the title "The Normative Structure of Science.")

Miller, Fred D., Jr. (1974) "Aristotle on the Reality of Time," *Archiv für Geschichte der Philosophie,* **56**: 132–155.

Miller, William B., Jr., František Baluška, and Arthur S. Reber (2023) "A Revised Central Dogma for the 21st Century: All Biology is Cognitive Information Processing," *Progress in Biophysics and Molecular Biology,* **182**: 34–48.

Mohseni, Masoud, Yasser Omar, Gregory S. Engel, and Martin B. Plenio, eds. (2014) *Quantum Effects in Biology.* Cambridge: Cambridge University Press.

Monds, Russell D. and George A. O'Toole (2008) "Metabolites as Intercellular Signals for Regulation of Community-Level Traits," in Stephen C. Winans and Bonnie L. Bassler, eds., *Chemical Communication Among Bacteria.* Washington, DC: ASM Press; pp. 105–129.

Montesquieu, Charles-Louis de Secondat, Baron de (1989) *The Spirit of the Laws,* translated and edited by Anne M. Cohler, Basia C. Miller, and Harold S. Stone. Cambridge: Cambridge University Press. (Originally published as *De l'esprit des loix*: Geneva: Barrillot & Fils, 1748.)

Montévil, Maël, Matteo Mossio, Arnaud Pocheville, and Giuseppe Longo (2016) "Theoretical Principles for Biology: Variation," *Progress in Biophysics and Molecular Biology,* **122**: 36–50.

Moore, G.E. (1993) "A Defence of Common Sense," in *G.E. Moore: Selected Writings,* edited by Thomas Baldwin. Oxford: Routledge; pp. 106–133. (Originally published in J.H. Muirhead, ed., *Contemporary British Philosophy: Personal Statements,* second series. London: George Allen and Unwin, 1925; pp. 193–223.)

Moosavi, Parisa (2018) "Neo-Aristotelian Naturalism and the Evolutionary Objection: Rethinking the Relevance of Empirical Science," in John Hacker-Wright, ed., *Philippa Foot on Goodness and Virtue.* London: Palgrave; pp. 277–307.

Moosavi, Parisa (2019) "From Biological Functions to Natural Goodness," *Philosophers' Imprint,* **19**: 1–20.

Moosavi, Parisa (2020) "Is the Neo-Aristotelian Concept of Organism Presupposed in Biology?," in Martin Hähnel, ed., *Aristotelian Naturalism: A Research Companion.* Cham, Switzerland: Springer International Publishing AG; pp. 329–342.

Moosavi, Parisa (2022a) "Natural Goodness without Natural History," *Philosophy and Phenomenological Research,* **104**: 78–100.

Moosavi, Parisa (2022b) "Neo-Aristotelian Naturalism as Ethical Naturalism," *Journal of Moral Philosophy,* **19**: 335–360.

Moreno, Alvaro and Matteo Mossio (2015) *Biological Autonomy: A Philosophical and Theoretical Enquiry.* Dordrecht, Netherlands: Springer.

Morrison, Margaret (2006) "Emergence, Reduction, and Theoretical Principles: Rethinking Fundamentalism," *Philosophy of Science,* **73**: 876–887.

Moss, Lenny (2003) *What Genes Can't Do.* Cambridge, MA: Bradford Books/MIT Press.

Mossio, Matteo, Maël Montévil, and Giuseppe Longo (2016) "Theoretical Principles for Biology: Organization," *Progress in Biophysics and Molecular Biology*, **122**: 24–35.

Murray, Charles (1984) *Losing Ground: American Social Policy, 1950–1980.* New York: Basic Books.

Murray, Charles (2012) *Coming Apart: The State of White America, 1960–2010.* New York: Crown Forum.

Myin, Erik and Farid Zahnoun (2018) "Reincarnating the Identity Theory," *Frontiers in Psychology*, **9**: 2044; doi:10.3389/fpsyg.2018.02044.

Nāgārjuna (2009) *A Strand of Dharma Jewels,* revised edition, translated by Bhikshu Dharmamitra. Seattle: Kalavinka Press.

Nagel, Thomas (2001) *The Last Word.* New York: Oxford University Press.

Nagel, Thomas (2012) *Mind and Cosmos: Why the Materialist Neo-Darwinian Conception of Nature is Almost Certainly False.* New York: Oxford University Press.

Newen, Albert, Leon De Bruin, and Shaun Gallagher, eds. (2018) *The Oxford Handbook of 4E Cognition.* Oxford: Oxford University Press.

Niklas, Karl J. and A. Keith Dunker (2016) "Alternative Splicing, Intrinsically Disordered Proteins, Calmodulin, and the Evolution of Multicellularity," in Karl J. Niklas and Stuart A. Newman, eds., *Multicellularity: Origins and Evolution.* Cambridge, MA: MIT Press; pp. 17–39.

Nivison, David S. (1996a) "Motivation and Moral Action in Mencius," in *idem, The Ways of Confucianism: Investigations in Chinese Philosophy,* edited by Bryan W. Van Norden. La Salle, IL: Open Court; pp. 91–119.

Nivison, David S. (1996b) "Golden Rule Arguments in Chinese Moral Philosophy," in *idem, The Ways of Confucianism: Investigations in Chinese Philosophy,* edited by Bryan W. Van Norden. La Salle, IL: Open Court; pp. 59–76.

Noble, Denis (2017) Dance *to the Tune of Life: Biological Relativity.* Cambridge: Cambridge University Press.

Noble, Raymond and Denis Noble (2021) "Can Reasons and Values Influence Action: How Might Intentional Agency Work Physiologically?," *Journal for General Philosophy of Science*, **52**: 277–295.

Norton, David L. (1991). *Democracy and Moral Development: A Politics of Virtue*. Berkeley, CA: University of California Press.

Novotný, Daniel D. (2013) Ens rationis *from Suárez to Caramuel: A Study in Scholasticism of the Baroque Era*. New York: Fordham University Press.

Novotný, Daniel D. (2019) "Suárez on Beings of Reason," *Conimbricenses.org Encyclopedia*, edited by Mário Santiago de Carvalho and Simone Guidi; doi:10.5281/zenodo.3571356.

Ockham, William (1974) *Ockham's Theory of Terms: Part 1 of the* Summa Logicae, translated by Michael J. Loux. Notre Dame, IN: University of Notre Dame Press. (The *Summa logicae* was composed around 1323.)

O'Connor, Timothy (2009) "Agent-Causal Power," in Toby Handfield, ed., *Dispositions and Causes*. Oxford: Oxford University Press; pp. 189–214.

Oderberg, David S. (2008) *Real Essentialism*. Abingdon, UK: Routledge.

Overgaard, Morten and Jesper Mogensen (2021) "Will We Explain Consciousness When We Find the Neural Correlates of Consciousness?," in Morten Overgaard, Jesper Mogensen, and Asger Kirkeby-Hinrup, eds., *Beyond Neural Correlates of Consciousness*. London: Routledge; pp. 4–15.

Paolini Paoletti, Michele (2016) "How I (Freely) Raised My Arm. Downward, Structural, Substance Causation," *Mind and Matter*, **12**: 203–228.

Peirce, Charles S. (1992a) "Some Consequences of Four Incapacities," in *idem, The Essential Peirce: Selected Philosophical Writings, Volume 1 (1867–1893)*, edited by Nathan Houser and Christian Kloesel. Bloomington: Indiana University Press; pp. 28–55. (Originally published in *Journal of Speculative Philosophy*, 1868, **2**: 140–157.)

Peirce, Charles S. (1992b) "The Doctrine of Necessity Examined," in *idem, The Essential Peirce: Selected Philosophical Writings, Volume 1 (1867–1893),* edited by Nathan Houser and Christian Kloesel. Bloomington: Indiana University Press; pp. 292–311. (Originally published in *The Monist*, 1892, **2**: 321–337.)

Peter of Spain (2014) *Summaries of Logic,* edited and translated by Brian P. Copenhaver, with Calvin Normore and Terence Parsons. Oxford: Oxford University Press. (Originally composed under the title *Tractatus,* most likely during the second quarter of the thirteenth century, this work later became known as *Summulae logicales.*)

Pieper, Josef (1966) *The Four Cardinal Virtues.* Notre Dame, IN: University of Notre Dame Press.

Pieper, Josef (1997) *Faith, Hope, Love.* San Francisco: Ignatius Press.

Pittendrigh, Colin S. (1958) "Adaptation, Natural Selection, and Behavior," in Anne Roe and George Gaylord Simpson, eds., *Behavior and Evolution.* New Haven, CT: Yale University Press, 1958; pp. 390–416.

Plaks, Andrew, trans. (2003) *Ta Hsüeh and Chung Yung.* London: Penguin Books.

Plato (1986) *Plato's Statesman,* translated with commentary by Seth Benardete. Chicago: University of Chicago Press. (*Plato's Statesman* is the third in a trilogy of translations, along with the *Theaetetus* and the *Sophist,* to which Benardete gave the collective name, *The Being of the Beautiful.*)

Plato (2001) *Plato's "Symposium,"* translated by Seth Benardete. Chicago: University of Chicago Press.

Pollack, Gerald H. (2001) *Cells, Gels and the Engines of Life: A New Unifying Approach to Cell Function.* Seattle, WA: Ebner & Sons.

Pollack, Gerald H. (2013) *The Fourth Phase of Water: Beyond Solid, Liquid, Vapor.* Seattle, WA: Ebner & Sons.

Popenoe, David (1996) *Life Without Father: Compelling New Evidence That Fatherhood and Marriage Are Indispensable for the Good of Children and Society.* Cambridge, MA: Harvard University Press.

Popper, Karl (1972) *Objective Knowledge: An Evolutionary Approach.* Oxford: Oxford University Press.

Popper, Karl (1982) "Introduction: Quantum Mechanics without "The Observer," in *idem, Quantum Theory and the Schism in Physics,* edited by W.W. Bartley, III. Totowa, NJ: Rowman & Littlefield, pp. 35–95. (Originally published in Mario Bunge, ed., *Quantum Theory and Reality,* Berlin: Springer Verlag, 1967, pp. 7–44.)

Porro, Pasquale (2001) "Angelic Measures: *aevum* and Discrete Time," in *idem,* ed., *The Medieval Concept of Time: Studies on the Scholastic Debate and Its Reception in Early Modern Philosophy.* Leiden: Brill; pp. 131–159.

Prior, Arthur N. (1970) "The Notion of the Present," *Studium Generale,* **23**: 245–248.

Proust, Marcel (2003) *In Search of Lost Time,* six volumes, translated by C.K. Scott Moncrieff, revised by Terence Kilmartin and D.J. Enright. New York: Modern Library. (Originally published as *À la recherche du temps perdu,* in seven volumes, Paris: Bernard Grasset et Gallimard, 1913–1927; note that the English translation was formerly known as *Remembrance of Things Past.*)

Radovan, Mario (2015) "On the Nature of Time"; https://arxiv.org/pdf/1509.01498.

Radovan, Mario (2024) "Dimensions of Reality"; DOI:10.13140/RG.2.2.32390.38729.

Raichle, Marcus E. (2010) "Two Views of Brain Function," *Trends in Cognitive Sciences,* **14**: P180–P190.

Raichle, Marcus E. (2015) "The Restless Brain: How Intrinsic Activity Organizes Brain Function," *Philosophical Transactions of the Royal Society B,* **370**(1668): 20140172.

Rasmussen, Douglas B. and Douglas J. Den Uyl (2005) *Norms of Liberty: A Perfectionist Basis for Non-Perfectionist Politics.* University Park, PA: Pennsylvania State University Press.

Rawls, John (1971) *A Theory of Justice.* Cambridge, MA: Belknap Press/Harvard University Press. (Revised edition: 1999.)

Rawls, John (1997) "The Idea of Public Reason Revisited," *University of Chicago Law Review,* **64**: 765–807.

Read, Catherine and Agnes Szokoloszky (2020) "Ecological Psychology and Enactivism: Perceptually-Guided Action vs. Sensation-Based Enaction," *Frontiers in Psychology*, **11**: article 1270.

Reid, Thomas (1997) *An Inquiry into the Human Mind on the Principles of Common Sense*, edited by Derek R. Brookes. University Park, PA: Pennsylvania State University Press. (First edition: Edinburgh: A. Kincaid and J. Bell, 1764.)

Reid, Thomas (2002) *Essays on the Intellectual Powers of Man*, edited by Derek R. Brookes. University Park, PA: Pennsylvania State University Press. (First edition: Edinburgh: John Bell, 1785.)

Reinach, Adolf (2012) *The Apriori Foundations of the Civil Law*. Frankfurt: ontos verlag. (Originally published as "Die apriorischen Grundlage des bürgerlichen Rechts," *Jahrbuch für Philosophie und phänomenologische Forschung*, 1913, **1**: 685–847.)

Rescher, Nicholas (2005) *Common-Sense: A New Look at an Old Philosophical Tradition*. Milwaukee, WI: Marquette University Press.

Riley, Patrick (2000) *Civilizing Sex: On Chastity and the Common Good*. Edinburgh: T&T Clark.

Robinson, Daniel N. (2002) *Praise and Blame: Moral Realism and Its Applications*. Princeton, NJ: Princeton University Press.

Rommen, Heinrich (1998) *Natural Law: A Study in Legal and Social History and Philosophy*. Indianapolis, IN: Liberty Fund. (Reprint of first, expanded, English edition: St. Louis, MO: B. Herder Book Co., 1948; originally published as *Die ewige Wiederkehr des Naturrechts*. Leipzig: Jakob Hegner, 1936.)

Roselli, Andrea and Christopher Austin (2021) "The Dynamical Essence of Powers," *Synthese*, **199**: 14951–14973.

Rosen, Robert (1991) *Life Itself: A Comprehensive Inquiry into the Nature, Origin, and Fabrication of Life*. New York: Columbia University Press.

Ross, James F. (2008) *Thought and World: The Hidden Necessities*. Notre Dame, IN: University of Notre Dame Press.

Rosslenbroich, Bernd, Susanna Kümmel, and Benjamin Bembé (forthcoming) "Agency as an Inherent Property of Living Organisms," *Biological Theory,* DOI: 10.1007/s13752-024-00471-7.

Russell, Daniel C. (2007) *Practical Intelligence and the Virtues.* Oxford: Clarendon Press.

Ryn, Claes G. (1994) "Virtue: Real and Imagined," in James E. Person, Jr., ed., *The Unbought Grace of Life: Essays in Honor of Russell Kirk.* Peru, IL: Sherwood Sugden and Company; pp. 115–136.

Sanders, Robert D., Giulio Tononi, Steven Laureys, and Jamie Sleigh (2012) "Unresponsiveness ≠ Unconsciousness," *Anesthesiology,* **116**: 946–959.

Sanson, David and Ben Caplan (2010) "The Way Things Were," *Philosophy and Phenomenological Research,* **81**: 24–39.

Śāntideva (1995) *The Bodhicaryāvatāra,* translated by Kate Crosby and Andrew Skilton. Oxford: Oxford University Press. (The Sanskrit original dates to around the first half of the eighth century AD; multiple translations into Tibetan, Chinese, and other languages.)

Satz, Helmut (2020) *The Rules of the Flock: Self-Organization and Swarm Structure in Animal Societies.* Oxford: Oxford University Press.

Sax, Leonard (2016) *The Collapse of Parenting: How We Hurt Our Kids When We Treat Them Like Grown-Ups.* New York: Basic Books.

Scheler, Max (1973) *Formalism in Ethics and Non-Formal Ethics of Values.* Evanston, IL: Northwestern University Press. (Originally published as *Der Formalismus in der Ethik und die matierale Wertethik.* Halle (Saale): M. Niemeyer, 1913.)

Schroeder, Frederic M. (2014) "From Alexander of Aphrodisias to Plotinus," in Pauliina Remes and Svetla Slaveva-Griffin, eds., *The Routledge Handbook of Neoplatonism.* Abingdon, UK: Routledge; pp. 293–309.

Schroeder, Frederic M. and Robert B. Todd, trans. (1990) *Two Greek Aristotelian Commentators on the Intellect.* Toronto: Pontifical Institute of Medieval Studies.

Sellars, Wilfrid (1963) "Empiricism and the Philosophy of Mind," in *idem, Science, Perception and Reality.* London: Routledge and Kegan Paul, pp. 127–196. (Originally published in Herbert Feigl and Michael Scriven, eds., *Minnesota Studies in the Philosophy of Science, vol. 1.* Minneapolis: University of Minnesota Press, 1956; pp. 253–329.)

Seneca, Lucius Annaeus (1995) "On Favours," in *idem, Moral and Political Essays,* edited and translated by John M. Cooper and J.F. Procopé. Cambridge: Cambridge University Press; 181–308.

Shapiro, James A. (2011) *Evolution: A View from the 21st Century.* Upper Saddle River, NJ: FT Science Press.

Shapiro, James A. (2021) "All Living Cells Are Cognitive," *Biochemical and Biophysical Research Communications,* **564**: 134–149.

Shapiro, James A. and Martin Dworkin, eds. (1997) *Bacteria as Multicellular Organisms.* Oxford: Oxford University Press.

Sher, George (1997) *Beyond Neutrality: Perfectionism and Politics.* Cambridge: Cambridge University Press.

Sher, George (2006) *In Praise of Blame.* New York: Oxford University Press.

Shulman, Robert G. (2013) *Brain Imaging: What It Can (and Cannot) Tell Us About Consciousness.* Oxford: Oxford University Press.

Skarda, Christine A. and Walter J. Freeman (1987) "How Brains Make Chaos in Order to Make Sense of the World," *Behavioral and Brain Sciences,* **10**:161–195.

Skewes, Joshua C. and Clifford A. Hooker (2009) "Bio-agency and the Problem of Action," *Biology and Philosophy,* **24**: 283–300.

Smith, Adam (1759) *The Theory of Moral Sentiments.* London: A. Millar. (Reprinted frequently, notably by Cambridge University Press, edited by Knud Haakonssen, in 2002.)

Soto, Ana, Giuseppe Longo, Maël Montévil, and Carlos Sonnenschein (2016a) "The Biological Default State of Cell Proliferation with Variation and Motility, A Fundamental Principle for a Theory of Organisms," *Progress in Biophysics and Molecular Biology,* **122**: 16–23.

Soto, Ana, Giuseppe Longo, Paul-Antoine Miquel, Maël Montévil, Matteo Mossio, Nicole Perret, Arnaud Pocheville, and Carlos Sonnenschein (2016b) "Toward a Theory of Organisms: Three Founding Principles in Search of a Useful Integration," *Progress in Biochemistry and Molecular Biology,* **122**: 77–82.

Sowell, Thomas (1995) *The Vision of the Anointed: Self-congratulation as a Basis for Social Policy.* New York: Basic Books.

Spencer, Herbert (1937) *First Principles,* sixth and final edition, revised by the author. London: Watts and Co. (First edition: London: Williams and Norgate, 1862; the sixth edition was first published in 1900.)

Spivey, Michael J. (2020) *Who You Are: The Science of Connectedness.* Cambridge, MA: MIT Press.

Steward, Helen (2012) *A Metaphysics for Freedom.* Oxford: Oxford University Press.

Stewart, John, Olivier Gapenne, and Ezequiel A. Di Paolo, eds. (2010) *Enaction: Toward a New Paradigm for Cognitive Science.* Cambridge, MA: Bradford Books/MIT Press.

Strawson, P.F. (1985) *Skepticism and Naturalism: Some Varieties.* New York: Columbia University Press.

Sultan, Sonia E., Armin P. Moczek, and Denis M. Walsh (2022) "Bridging the Explanatory Gaps: What Can We Learn from a Biological Agency Perspective?," *BioEssays,* **44**: article 2100185.

Swanson, Paul L. (2018) "Karma Made Me Do It: A Buddhist Take on Consciousness and Free Will," in *idem, In Search of Clarity: Essays on Translation and Tiantai Buddhism.* Nagoya, Japan: Chisokudo; pp. 167–181.

Tallant, Jonathan (2009) "Ontological Cheats Might Just Prosper," *Analysis,* **69**: 422–430.

Tertullian (1993) "The Five Books Against Marcion" in Alexander Roberts and James Donaldson, eds., *The Ante-Nicene Fathers: Volume III: Latin Christianity: Its Founder, Tertullian,* reprint edition. Grand Rapids, MI: Wm. B. Eerdmans Publishing Co.; pp. 269–475. (Original publication: Edinburgh: T. & T. Clark. 1874.)

Thompson, Evan (2007) *Mind in Life: Biology, Phenomenology, and the Sciences of Mind.* Cambridge, MA: Belknap Press/Harvard University Press.

Thompson, Michael (2008) *Life and Action: Elementary Structures of Practice and Practical Thought.* Cambridge, MA: Harvard University Press.

Timpe, Kevin (2017) "Leeway vs. Sourcehood Conceptions of Free Will," in Kevin Timpe, Meghan Griffith, and Neil Levy, eds., *The Routledge Companion to Free Will.* New York: Routledge; pp. 213–224.

Tu Weiming (1991) "Afterword: Thinking of 'Enlightenment' Religiously," in Peter N. Gregory, ed., *Sudden and Gradual: Approaches to Enlightenment in Chinese Thought.* Delhi: Motilal Banarsidass Publishers; pp. 447–456. (First edition: Honolulu: University of Hawaii Press, 1987.)

Turvey, Michael T. (2019) *Lectures on Perception: An Ecological Perspective.* New York: Routledge.

Van Cleve, James (1999) *Problems from Kant.* Oxford: Oxford University Press.

Van Duijn, Marc, Fred Keijzer, and Daan Franken (2006) "Principles of Minimal Cognition: Casting Cognition as Sensorimotor Coordination," *Adaptive Behavior,* **14**: 157–170.

van Gelder, Timothy (1995) "What Might Cognition Be, If Not Computation?," *Journal of Philosophy,* **92**: 345–381.

Villon, François (2014) *Oeuvres complètes,* edited by Jacqueline Cerquiglini-Toulet. Paris: Gallimard. (*Le Testament* was composed around 1461 and was first published posthumously in 1489.)

Vitiello, Giuseppe (2001) *My Double Unveiled: The Dissipative Quantum Model of Brain.* Amsterdam: John Benjamins Publishing Co.

Von Bodman, Susanne B., Joanne M. Willey, and Stephen P. Diggle (2008) "Cell-Cell Communication in Bacteria: United We Stand," *Journal of Bacteriology,* **190**: 4377–4391.

Voosholz, Jan and Markus Gabriel, eds. (2021) *Top-Down Causation and Emergence.* Cham, Switzerland: Springer Nature.

Wagman, Jeffrey B. and Julia J.C. Blau, eds. (2019) *Perception as Information Detection: Reflections on Gibson's Ecological Approach to Visual Perception.* New York: Routledge.

Walsh, Denis M. (2015) *Organisms, Agency, and Life.* Cambridge: Cambridge University Press.

Walsh, Denis M. and Gregory Rupik (2023) "The Agential Perspective: Countermapping the Modern Synthesis," *Evolution and Development,* **25**: 335–352.

Warnock, Mary (1976) *Imagination.* London: Faber & Faber.

Washington, George (1997) *Writings,* edited by John Rhodehamel. New York: The Library of America. (The First Inaugural Address was delivered to a joint session of Congress on April 30, 1789.)

Watterson, John G. (2018) "In Search of a Physics of Cytoplasm," *Water: A Multidisciplinary Research Journal,* **10**: 1–10.

Watterson, John G. (in progress) "Thales' Legacy"; website: thewaterpixel.com.

Wedin, Michael V. (1988) *Mind and Imagination in Aristotle.* New Haven, CT: Yale University Press.

West-Eberhard, Mary Jane (2003) *Developmental Plasticity and Evolution.* Oxford: Oxford University Press.

Whitehead, Alfred North (1978*) Process and Reality: An Essay in Cosmology,* corrected edition, edited by David Ray Griffin and Donald W. Sherburne. New York: Free Press. (Originally published by Cambridge University Press in 1929.)

Williams, Neil E. (2019) *The Powers Metaphysic.* Oxford: Oxford University Press.

Williams, Richard N. and Daniel N. Robinson, eds. (2015) *Scientism: The New Orthodoxy.* London: Bloomsbury Academic.

Wilson, James Q. (1993) *The Moral Sense.* New York: Free Press.

Wilson, James Q. (2002) *The Marriage Problem: How Our Culture Has Weakened Families.* New York: HarperCollins.

Withagen, Rob and John van der Kamp (2010) "Towards a New Ecological Conception of Perceptual Information: Lessons from a Developmental Systems Perspective," *Human Movement Science,* **29**: 149–163.

Xenophon (1994) *Memorabilia*, translated and annotated by Amy L. Bonnette. Ithaca, NY: Cornell University Press.

Xunzi (2003) *Basic Writings*, translated by Burton Watson. New York: Columbia University Press.

Yates, F. Eugene, ed. (1987) *Self-Organizing Systems: The Emergence of Order.* New York: Plenum Press.

Yates, F. Eugene (1994) "Order and Complexity in Dynamical Systems: Homeodynamics as a Generalized Mechanics for Biology," *Mathematical and Computer Modeling*, **19**(6–8): 49–74.

Yuste, Rafael, Jason N. MacLean, Jeffrey Smith, and Anders Lansner (2005) "The Cortex as a Central Pattern Generator," *Nature Reviews Neuroscience*, **6**: 477–483.

Zahnoun, Farid (2020) "Explaining the Reified Notion of Representation from a Linguistic Perspective," *Phenomenology and the Cognitive Sciences*, **19**: 79–96.

Zahnoun, Farid (2021a) "The Socio-Normative Nature of Representation," *Adaptive Behavior*, **29**: 417–429.

Zahnoun, Farid (2021b) "On Representation Hungry Cognition (and Why We Should Stop Feeding It)," *Synthese*, **198** (Supp. 1): S267–S284.

Index

www.ingramcontent.com/pod-product-compliance
Lightning Source LLC
Chambersburg PA
CBHW060144130626
46556CB00006B/2493